OBSERVATIONS ON
MODERN FALCONRY

BY

R. STEVENS

British Library Cataloguing-in-Publication Data
A catalogue record for this book is available from the
British Library

CONTENTS

Falconry

'Falconry' refers to the hunting of wild quarry in its natural state and habitat by means of a trained bird of prey. There are two traditional terms used to describe a person involved in falconry: a 'falconer' flies a falcon, and an 'austringer' (a term of German origin) flies a hawk or an eagle. Falconry has a long and distinguished history, and it has been suggested that it began in Mesopotamia, with the earliest accounts dating to approximately 2000 BC. It was probably introduced to Europe around 400 AD however, when the Huns and the Alans invaded from the East. Frederick II of Hohenstaufen (a member of the Swabian dynasty in the High Middle Ages who possessed huge amounts of territory across Europe) is generally acknowledged as the most significant wellspring of traditional falconry knowledge. He is believed to have obtained firsthand knowledge of Arabic falconry during wars in the region in 1228 and 1229, in which he participated in his role as Holy Roman Emperor. Frederick is best known for his falconry treatise, *De Arte Venandi Cum Avibus* (The Art of Hunting with Birds); the first comprehensive book on falconry, as well as a substantial contribution to ornithology and zoology. Historically, falconry has always been a popular sport of the upper classes and nobility, largely due to the

1

prerequisites of time, money and space. However, within some societies, such as the Bedouin, falconry was not practiced for recreation, but for purely practical reasons of supplementing a very limited diet. In the UK, falconry reached its zenith in the seventeenth century, but faded reasonably rapidly due to the introduction of firearms for hunting in the eighteenth and nineteenth centuries. It did witness a revival in the late nineteenth and earlier twentieth centuries however, when several falconry books were published. Interestingly, in early English falconry literature, the word 'falcon' referred to a female falcon only, while the word 'hawk' referred to a female hawk. A male hawk or falcon was referred to as a 'tercel', as it was roughly one third less than the female in size. Whilst falconry is now practiced in many countries world wide, it is less common in areas such as Australasia. In Australia, although falconry is not specifically illegal, it is illegal to keep any type of bird of prey in captivity without the appropriate permits, and in New Zealand, falconry was legalised for one species only, the Swap/Australasian harrier, in 2011. There are currently only four practicing falconers in New Zealand. However, in countries such as the UK and US today, falconry is experiencing a boom. Its popularity, through lure flying displays at country houses and game fairs, has probably never been higher in the past 300 years. It has also been the subject of a popular book *Falcon Fever*, written by Tim Gallagher in 2008. Falconry is also used for practical purposes in the modern day, the birds are taught to control other pest birds and animals in urban areas, landfills, commercial buildings, and even airports.

FOREWORD

THERE are quite a number of modern books on Falconry, written within the last hundred years, so I feel a little diffident in adding yet another one. Their authors write all that is necessary to put the beginner on the right road, so it would seem that there is nothing more to add. Nevertheless, I daresay that most falconers find much to puzzle over and much to widen their interest as they progress. It is on such matters of which much of the substance is not found on the beaten track of text-book Falconry, that I have attempted to write. I have written this book not because of any wish to be controversial, not because I expect acceptance of any expressed opinion, but simply because anyone who has practised Falconry for as long as I have may be excused for writing his conclusions. No mistaken sense of duty has driven me to it, only the sheer pleasure of writing about a sport that has so completely captivated me.

One does not need to be particularly intelligent to have absorbed quite a lot of knowledge after flying hawks for over thirty seasons as I have done. I trust that I have brought a little refreshment to the subject though I fear that nothing has been added that is new. Nevertheless perhaps something has been shed over these pages that will help a beginner with an equally unquenchable thirst as my own for finding out more about the Peregrine in her relationship to modern Falconry.

Reasons of economy have necessitated the omission of illustrations. The book is strictly "utility," that is why most of the romantic falconry terms have been left out and falcons have been called hawks. Opinions have been stripped of the customary verbal wrappings that modesty demands, but for that perhaps I may be forgiven under the plea that I have tried to keep strictly to business. If contemporary falconers find these opinions unduly provocative I hope they will allow that there are so many conflicting ones inside the Ancient Art that no falconer need be backward in asserting his own.

I am grateful to those friends who, through word of mouth and by correspondence, are always ready to share with me what experience has revealed to them. Their help has been invaluable. This is a good opportunity to thank them, and that I do, most sincerely.

THE MEWS

A TRAINED hawk's housing requirements are simple. Her primary need is shelter from the wind, rain and snow. After that she appreciates dryness, fresh air and an absence of draught. They are exactly the conditions that a wild hawk seeks. Happily we can provide them for our trained ones, and the nearer to completion they are the more the hawks will benefit in health and comfort.

There have to be variations of course. A newly-caught hawk cannot be put into a mews that has daylight inside. Neither should her owner wish to incarcerate her in darkness when she has become tame. So a mews must be adaptable to suit an untrained and a trained hawk.

At the time of writing these lines it is a day of gales and driving rain. My hawks, longwings, are in their mews sitting in full daylight, or such of it as the murky clouds allow to come through. Each one has its foot drawn up. The rain and the wind do not drive in because corrugated-iron sheeting, higher and wider than the mews and erected five feet away from it to allow easy passage, protects the wide-open door. This same sheeting prevents their seeing the outside world, which, on the dawn of anything like a fine day, would otherwise beckon them to fly out, an invitation to which they could, and would, only reply by bating and jumping against their jesses. They are now sitting perfectly still in such contentment as a non-flying day permits them. The downpipes from the gutters on the roof run the rainwater into drains, and there is no creeping wetness in the sand on the mews floor because the whole structure is raised on a concrete base.

The interior of the mews is severely plain. It has no beam nor ledge to tempt a hawk to fly to a higher perching place. Anything that appears to offer a foothold above her rightful perch holds a hawk's attention. For weeks, months perhaps, she cannot keep her eye off it. Ultimately she ceases to pay it attention, but the experience is hurtful because it takes an awful lot of bating and jumping against her jesses before she learns so hardly that she cannot get there. And it is vexatious to her to have this quite unnecessary and forbidding hand of restriction keeping her down. In a well-ordered mews a hawk sits at ease because there is no other inviting perching place in it to sharpen that inherent hankering, characteristic of the birds of prey, for a higher pinnacle from which to survey their surroundings. Her perch is at about the level of the falconer's shoulder, which is as high as convenient to put her on and take her off it. This she accepts because it is the height of her contentment.

How often does a beginner in Falconry, on hearing the *jiggety-jiggety* of his hawk's bells in the mews, try to dismiss it from his mind as nothing more than the restlessness of a partly-trained bird seeking freedom? He consoles himself in the thought that only more training and more time is required to put the condition right. If he only but knew that the fretting could be corrected that same day by the removal, or screening off, of the particular beam or ledge, or ray of light or patch of sunlight, that all the time, his hawk is trying to reach, and not the larger freedom of the outer world as he mistakenly believes!

A mews should not be so wide as to leave extensive floor space on either side of the perch which might cause a hawk to hang, frustrated, in her efforts to reach it. Sometimes it is convenient to have two perches, one on either side, each being sufficiently far from the wall to prevent wing-tips reaching it, and far enough from the opposite perch to allow the falconer easy passage between the two, so that a hawk, bating from his fist, will not reach either of them. They must be on the same level, and, so as to obviate as much risk as possible of a hawk's attempting to fly to the opposite perch, the mews interior should be painted black and the padding on the perches should be of the same colour so that by its inconspicuousness each perch carries no invitation to attempt a hop across. I have always found this plan to work satisfactorily.

A mews should be sufficiently high for the perch to be well away from the roof, for it is immediately under the roof that the worst air collects. Apart from this a hawk's raised wing-tips should never be able to brush the roof's underside.

When an already existing shed has to be converted to a mews, all beams, projections, etc. can be hidden from the hawk by hanging strips of hessian. If there is too much floor space in front of the perch it can be narrowed by the same device. All such hanging material must be made fast, however, so that it cannot disturb a hawk by agitation from air currents.

As a precaution against the entry of a stray dog or cat into an open mews it is a good plan to have an outer, skeleton door with narrow, vertical bars that will obstruct as little as possible the inflow of fresh air, yet accurately gauged to prevent a squeeze-through of a hawk should she free herself from the screen-perch.

This open, fresh-air-filled mews that I have described keeps hawks in better health and greater contentment and with sharper appetites than the tightly-shut dark mews that tradition has ordained. Yet the former must be convertible to the latter, of course, when newly-caught hack hawks, passagers or haggards, have to be dealt with. As the tameness of new hawks increases, and as the mews interior becomes more familiar to them, they can be allowed more light and fresh air in progressive stages. The falconer's ultimate aim should be to have his hawks breathing equally good air inside and outside, to arrange his mews so that it is for them a house of rest and not of fidgets. Everything must be calculated to persuade them to rest inside with the same repose and comfort that the wild hawk enjoys in her own home rocks.

It is sometimes said that a trained hawk would rather jowk outside, free, even on a dirty night than be taken into a mews where everything has been studied for her comfort. That may be true of certain individuals but I would challenge that statement when applied to really tame ones.

I have an intermewed eyass Gyr tiercel, a bird of Arctic regions that might be expected to regard our comparatively mild climate with scorn. This particular hawk sometimes gets left out on a grouse he has killed, but, unless fog cuts him off, he always returns home before nightfall. With a bulge still on his crop he allows me to take him up and carry him into the mews. If the day has been wild and wet he loses no time in closing his eyes once he feels the familiar perch under his feet, an unmistakable sign of contentment. Even in fine, calm weather he returns just the same. I do not doubt that it is his predilection for the mews at night that urges him to wing his way home over miles of moorland. The habit is not peculiar to him as eyass Peregrines have proved. His sister, too, has never yet failed to come home to roost.

As trained hawks spend about half their lives on the screen-perch this piece of furniture merits more study than it often gets. The illustrated mistake one sometimes sees in books on Falconry is of a perch with a single length of material hung on its underside. The regaining of her perch by a hawk that has bated off is an unnatural exercise that does her more harm than good. Why add to her difficulty, why give her an additional

11

obstacle to surmount in the step created unnecessarily by the perch's bulge over the single screen? And just to make it still harder work for her, the screen, if we are to follow these old illustrations, is to be attached only at intervals under the length of the perch so that, in between, gaps are formed between the underside of the perch and the top of the screen. After use of course the sag becomes greater and these gaps become deeper. Such obstacles do not defeat the hawk, in fact she gets very clever in performing her enforced acrobatics but why, why impose such an unnecessary strain on her back?

To reduce the fatigue of regaining the perch, after a bate, as much as possible, the screen must be put right *over* the perch so that it hangs down each side. Thus the perch's bulge is under cover and nullified so that a hawk can regain the perch with minimum effort, because her climb up is a straight one unimpeded by bulge or gap. The screen in all cases of course is heavily weighted at the bottom to hold it taut for the climbing hawk. When the screen is a double one, as advocated, and joined its entire length along the bottom like a roller towel, it is easy to lay iron rods inside. These should be continuous from end to end to give the screen its maximum tautness and to avoid ugly creases and folds.

A perch should be thick, not so thick as to catch any mute or prevent the clearance of the feet of the hawk that is bating off, but thick enough to allow a hawk on it to rest without any suspicion of a grip. (This refers to falcons not to shortwings).

Her spread toes should be as nearly on a level as practicable so that her weight is not concentrated on the ball of the foot. The top of the perch can be levelled off to some extent by planing off a little of the wood. When a wild hawk perches on a rock of her choice it will be observed that she uses her tail against it as an aid to balance, thus further distributing her weight. A screen-perch should enable a trained hawk to rest in the same stance as a wild one, that is why it should have a reasonably generous surface on top. If a perch is a slender one a hawk is compelled to sit at the perpendicular right down to the tip of her tail so as to preserve balance. Almost her entire weight is thus taken by the ball of the foot, to her discomfort. Where there is a tendency to corns and swollen feet this is one way to aggravate the condition.

WEATHERING ENCLOSURE -
BATH - BLOCKS

IN an ideal Falconry establishment the mews is either in or adjacent to the weathering enclosure. The weathering enclosure must be well drained and sheltered from wind which hawks hate when having to sit in it, so much so that it makes them bate continuously. It should be situated where it can get plenty of sunshine, particularly the early morning and the evening sunshine. A continuous, dense, high hedge is the best boundary with the top of the hedge spreading out, to give shade from a hot sun. If there is no hedge available then some kind of a ring fence will have to be strongly erected. This can be of wire netting if the situation is a sheltered one and there are trees in it to give shade. The netting should be six feet high to keep out dogs, and it will need in addition a turn-out at the top if there is a prowling cat about. But if the situation be exposed to wind then sheet-iron or wooden fencing will be required. Supporting posts should all be a few inches short of the top, otherwise hawks in the enclosure will fret themselves in trying to fly up onto them. If the trees in the enclosure are big ones the falconer will have to be careful about the risk of branches and sticks falling on his hawks in windy weather.

Quite a generous area is needed for a weathering enclosure.

A hawk's block has to be moved every day to fresh turf so that, as much as possible, her mutes are always being left behind in an endeavour to keep her as clear as one can from possible infection. It should be large enough for a low sun to shine on some part of its interior. It should be so large that the blocks can be moved two or three times daily on to clean ground so as to allow the falconer to move his hawks into the sun, or shade, or away from areas of falling branches.

An important feature of the weathering enclosure is the bath. I know of nothing better than a round concrete bath sunk in the ground with a turf edge to it. It should have a plug hole and drainage system as it is troublesome and difficult to make a good job of emptying it by scooping out the water. There should be a gradual slope from the edge to the middle, and, when the hawk has waded in, the water should come at least half-way up to her shoulders when she stands over the plug-hole. And when in the middle the tips of her extended wings should, of course, be in the water and well clear of the edge. Indeed the bath should be larger than what this indicates because a hawk is cautious in her approach to the "deep end" and likes to wade in on a gentle slope from the very shallow water at the edge.

A new hawk will enter a bath of this description days, occasionally weeks, before she will summon up enough courage to face a tin-pan contraption. It should of course be built where it receives the morning sun.

To avoid fouling the ground round the bath a hawk should be removed from the "bath block" if she does not enter the water within ten minutes, or soon after shaking herself on emergence.

The water should be changed as soon as it shows the least suspicion of a greasy film on it, and, needless to add the "bath block" should be at such a distance that no mute can get into the water.

As soon as a new hawk is accustomed to weathering, a good falconer will take her out of the mews early in the morning and she will not be returned to the screen perch until sundown. Only rain, hail or fog will keep her inside if the weathering enclosure is adequately protected from gales. Therefore as she spends so much of her time on the block we ought to give this important piece of furniture a lot of thought. Let us take "as read" details of the revolving iron ring which is indispensable for tying the end of the leash to and which is adequately described in the text books, and let us agree that the top of the block must provide ample room for the feet, yet not be so wide as to catch any mute or so narrow for the jesses to straddle its width so that the hawk gets pinned down at the base.

It is sometimes advocated that the top of a block be padded. Personally I disagree with this as padding holds the damp. I have never known a plain wooden top to produce corns. I have tried cork tops because cork dries more quickly than wood after rain, but cork perishes and chips off so I discontinued it.

It is necessary for the top of the block to be of greater circumference than the base, otherwise without this taper the leash will cling and get wrapped round the block as the hawk turns round. It also prevents mutes streaking the sides. But what really is important is the height of the block. Speaking generally the higher the block the greater the contentment of the hawk that rests on it. When a hawk in training is unhooded, on an eight-inch high block, for the first time, she loses very little time in bating off it. And also, far more often than not, she takes a long time before regaining it. It is so close to the ground that she hardly condescends to recognize it as a perching place. She gets accustomed to it in time, and some falconers become accustomed to seeing their hawks thus absurdly placed, while others rebel against having their hawks weathering with tails nearly brushing the grass.

I admit that a sixteen-inch high block is still far from the sort of resting place a hawk would naturally choose, but at least it does give her that modicum of elevation of which a new hawk is quick to take advantage.

I believe that hawks are all the better in health, certainly in morale, for being kept higher off the ground even though the difference be only an extra eight inches. Beside, appearances do count. It does seem a shame to detract from a falcon's dignity by putting her on the lower, when she looks twice the bird on the taller block.

It seems that the modern falconer is becoming increasingly aware of the desirability of tall blocks, so much so that blocks of up to five feet in height are to-day seen in some weathering enclosures, particularly in the United States. On one of these a Peregrine falcon, for instance, really is lifted up, literally, to something nearer resembling her rightful position. She is more on equal terms with the falconer when he approaches to take her up, an important psychological factor this, for on a low block a hawk dislikes the towering form of a man over her.

When a hawk bates off the old type block she gets exercise of a sort, though it is very doubtful whether it does her any good, but in regaining the top of a five-foot block she really does have to use her wings. That surely would assist to keep her muscles supple through the long months of moulting at the block.

In construction this new block differs from the old in that most of its height is taken up by an iron rod which goes into the ground and supports the block proper, into which it is spiked. Thus we have the real block at the top, only five or six inches or less in depth and sharply tapered. At the foot of the iron rod the leash is tied to a light iron ring which is pulled up the rod when the hawk bates off, thus easing her descent to the ground.

The following description is out of a letter from an American friend:—

"We do not use a low block if we can avoid it. On the lawn both the falcons and accipiters are perched on high blocks. These are blocks on a long rod, long enough so that the bird is about five feet from the ground. The leash is secured to a ring which is free to slide up and down the rod between the ground and the block. The leash is tied so that there is no slack, but still the ring is not half off the ground. This eliminates the danger of the bird wrapping the leash around the rod several times and fouling it. In using a high block, it is imperative that the jesses be short, otherwise there is the possibility of the bird straddling the block. Birds do less bating, because they appear happier with the height. There is less feather damage than with the bow perch or low block, and the birds can get more exercise in flying up to the block. When they bate the ring slides up to the block and this itself slows them somewhat. Then the rod gives some so that the strain on the legs is actually less than with the low block and a shorter leash. Everyone that I know that has tried the high block swears by them."

During the last summer I tried a modification of what might be called the American type block. Mine was three feet high above ground instead of five. I used a leash just over six feet in length so that it was not taut nor pulling on the hawk's legs. An iron plate was fixed on the pin of the block so that after pushing the spiked end of the pin into the ground the plate lay flat on the turf. The purpose of the plate was to give the block greater stability, and to ensure that the ring, lying on it, would have absolutely nothing to impede its ascent when the hawk bates off.

For many days after this block was put into use it was kept pretty constantly under observation, for it was feared that the hawk, on flying forward, might pull the leash over the top of the block, and, though the length of the leash was gauged so that the hawk could still reach ground on this happening, there was very little space for the hawk's comfort and her feathers would be in some danger through her being held so close to the pin of the block. To minimize this risk the top edge of the block had been rounded off and a round leather leash was used instead of a flat one. It was felt that a still longer leash would be undesirable because of the greater jerk the hawk would receive on being pulled up at the end of her bate. A deeper block on top of the pin was at first tried because it was thought that the hawk would prefer to have something more substantial to fly onto from the ground than the rather saucer-like affair of conventional pattern. However it soon had to be removed and a sharply tapered five-inch deep block substituted because it was found that the greater weight of the deeper block made too springy a foothold, held aloft on the pliant pin, every time the weight of the hawk came against it when she flew back onto it.

This block was used daily for three months without a mishap of any kind. The hawk took to it at once and seemed very pleased with it. It at once became obvious why a block perched up on a long pin was the only possible form a really high block could take, for had it been of wood from top to bottom there could not have been sufficient taper to prevent the leash from clinging and getting wrapped round it as the hawk turns. It was found that the leash always hung well away from the pin, and although it did occasionally coil round at the bottom, over the plate, the hawk never failed to pull it out again on bating. No doubt the large size of the ring, two and a half inch diameter, and the fact that the leash was round and fairly stiff, allowed this. And then again had the block been in the foim of a wooden post there would have been absolutely no give in it to a bating hawk. But by the pulling up of the iron ring the shock of a bate came against the top of the pin, just where it gave the greatest pliancy, thus reducing considerably the strain on the hawk's legs. I never knew an occasion when the ring did not run up the pin when the hawk bated.

The block worked perfectly, yet after three months I discarded it. Not so much because I could not rid myself of a lingering fear that something might happen to the hawk on it, as because, even at that modest height, the wind caught her too much, the belt of spruce planted round the weathering enclosure not having grown up sufficiently yet.

The sixteen-inch high block is not of an impressive height, but without doubt a hawk finds greater contentment on it than on one half that height, and it does keep her raised to some extent above those invisible, chilling vapours that cling to the ground on cold damp days.

BELLS—JESSES—CLIP SWIVELS
LURES—HOODS—WHISTLE

IN flying, the wild hawk always has one indisputable advantage over the trained one and that is she flies without any kind of encumbrance, whereas our own birds are impeded by jesses and bells. This impediment is, of course, slight, but it is a factor that we have to consider. In regard to the bells, all we can do is to ensure that they are as light as possible consistent with loud-ringing tone. Of course the "load" can be halved by putting on only one bell. One bell on one leg would hardly make any difference as far as the question of balance in flying and stooping is concerned, but the volume of sound produced would be halved and so the danger of losing a hawk would be increased, not only on that account, but also because a one-toned tinkle so often resembles other sounds in nature as, for example, the one-toned tinkling notes of meadow pipits which is such a common sound on heaths and moors where these little birds abound. When two bells are affixed, with one a semi-tone above the other, as they should be, the pleasant jangling discord produced is so unmistakeable that it cannot be associated with anything else than a hawk.

As far as I am aware no one has yet devised a method whereby jesses may be completely taken off a hawk before flight and put on again after the flight. All we can do is to keep them as short as possible, as narrow as possible and to use the thinnest leather consistent with a reasonable degree of strength. It would be foolish of course to put on jesses so slight as to run the risk of a hawk's breaking or biting through them. When a hawk is new one must be extra cautious in this respect. As times goes on, however, and it is found that she does not pull at her jesses, one can, with discretion, put on a narrower and possibly a thinner pair. They can be shorter too, but only when the hawk has become tame and steady, for there is hardly any experience more nerve-racking than taking up a shy hawk with short jesses. On "safe" Peregrine falcons I usually end up by using jesses that are four inches long measured from the loops round the legs to the swivel ends, and two-fifths of an inch in width or less. I do not believe in shaping jesses to give extra width round the legs, as it is objectionable to the hawk to encase her legs too much.

Apart from the additional encumbrance that long jesses create it must be borne in mind that they are a source of danger when the hawk is on the block. Their length allows them to fall each side of the top of the block so that when the hawk bates off her body completes the encitclement of the block and she is pinned down.

On the other hand if a hawk with short jesses be tied on the screen-perch in the orthodox way, that is to say with the swivel holding the ends of the jesses down on the perch, she is in even greater danger. The figure-eight swivel unfortunately rarely works as a swivel, or at least cannot be relied upon to do so, and so the hawk only has to turn round a few times to get twisted up. This of course makes her uncomfortable and so she continues to turn round, unfortunately always in the same direction. The twisted jesses constrict her legs so that by the morning she may have swollen feet. If the falconer is still more unfortunate he may find that she has been twisted right off the perch and hanging in an exhausted condition. In any case four inch jesses even without twisting, are far too short for comfort on the perch. This danger of short jesses on the perch can be averted by affixing to the figure-eight swivel another kind of swivel. For this purpose the smaller dog clip-swivels are excellent. A word of caution is, however, very necessary here. It is no use going into an ironmonger's shop and buying one small swivel for one hawk. Half a dozen will be needed and, even then, it may be found, on close examination, that only one is really safe to use. There are different kinds, qualities, and sizes of these dog clip-swivels on the market. Be sure that you see them all. Choose those that are not too big and heavy and only those with a firmly-closing strong spring. Those that open and close by means of a separate, flat, thin steel flange are no good. In the correct kind part of the thick steel rim itself presses inwards against a spring. Really strong fingers are needed to snap a suitable one onto the figure-eight swivel. Such cannot be opened by a hawk. When you do. snap it on, however, be sure to pull the jesses to make sure the two swivels are engaged. This is particularly necessary in an uncertain light.

In course of time the spring of a clip swivel may become weaker, a new swivel should then be substituted.

The clip swivel with its ring attachment will add another couple of inches to a hawk's jesses, and the two connecting swivels, the figure eight and the dog clip, will obviate the risk of the jesses becoming twisted up. The latter can be affixed to the perch by a staple.

All the way down through the centuries the accoutrements of Falconry have been bedizened and bedecked wherever possible. Jewelled hoods, silver varvels, silver bells, sumptuous gauntlets, reflected the glories of this sport of kings and princes whose falconers were attired in handsome gold-buttoned uniforms. There is not much we can do about this sort of thing nowadays, so that when modern young falconers put gay plumes on their hawks' hoods and produce lures ornamented with pretty feathers, they are showing the right spirit. Far be it from us to discourage their efforts with any prosy criticism. It may be permissible gently to point out that a mallard's, pheasant's, jay's, or magpie's wings cured with salt or alum may not be in the best interests of a hawk's health. One may even hint at the advisability of preventing a hungry hawk from getting her beak into an imperfectly preserved decaying pinion joint, then leave it at that.

26

It is often a long time before a young falconer learns that a meat-garnished lure is not a whit more attractive to a trained hawk for being decked out with a bird's preserved wings. These embellishments do no harm, of course, except when they become greasy and smelly through overmuch use, but, however artistically put on, however "birdy" they make the lure appear, the hawk is not fooled. The lure may be deftly twirled about, it may be thrown high into the air, and the hawk, with the utmost tenacity, will follow its twists and turns as though she were indeed trying to catch a bird. But should her human partner delude himself in the belief that she is so deceived, then it is he who is fooled, not the hawk.

The plain fact is that the lure is nothing more than an object with which the trained hawk learns to associate food, so we do well to strip it of conventional trappings and so make it easier to keep the thing clean. The strings on it should not be allowed to become smelly. It should be brightly coloured to facilitate finding it on the occasions when it gets dropped and lost.

On the subject of hoods, jewelled, plumed, here again I regret to appear in the ugly rôle of destroyer of cherished tradition. As a young man I used to buy hoods from Mollen at four and sixpence each. Without the jewels they were still things of beauty but, alas, not a joy forever, for after a few days the handsome green cloth, that covered the eye-pieces, became torn and tattered by the scratching of the hawks who evidently failed to appreciate it. They then got to work with their pounces on the attractive red, woollen bosses at the base of the plumes so that the wool became fluffed and untidy and got in the way of the beak-openings. After a few months the plumes, if they escaped being moth-eaten, became tired-looking with the dust and dirt that stuck to them and then they got broken and bent. Surveying all this wreckage that time always served up I fell into thinking how heavy these hoods were. To the hawks they must have felt about as comfortable as steel helmets did to the mediaeval knights.

While on the subject of weight I would like to mention a hood which Dr. Gordon Jolly once showed me. It was a hood which he had used while hawking in North Africa and was typical of those which the Arabs have made for centuries. It is very light in weight and simple in construction having a hanging leather thong instead of a plume, and no opening at the back. I mention this hood parenthetically because Dr. Jolly informs me that it is the ancestor of our Dutch hood which I have been criticising. This North African hood is basically of the same shape but has the advantage of a wider beak opening. It has much to commend it, though, to our way of thinking, is less practicable because it easily loses its shape, on account of the very light leather it is made from, and in use is less convenient because its back does not open.

Evidently I am not alone in condemning Dutch hoods for they seem to be going out of fashion nowadays while Indian type hoods are taking their place. The latter embody the only good feature of the former, *i.e.*, the openings and the braces at the back. Their peculiar shape results in a hood structurally strong enough for the employment of thinner and softer leather so that they have the great advantage of lightness. The beak opening is very much wider, avoiding contact with the soft parts of the beak, thus a hawk can eat freely through this hood, while it has some difficulty in doing so through the Dutch.

If the Indian hood be stained with bright colours it need not be far behind the Dutch in appearance. Its thonged tag which is further back and set at an attractive, rakish angle is in my opinion, as saucy as any feathered plume. It gives the hood a decidedly racy appearance. Actually, I have never met a falconer who, once he has got used to it, does not prefer this type of hood not only for its greater usefulness but for its looks too.

Every article of furniture and equipment is of such supreme importance that if the falconer fail to give any one of them his closest study he is not taking full advantage of the hawk's potentiality for the sport in which man and bird are partners. Of them all it is the hood, beyond doubt, that can give the greatest trouble. A good hood can never be anything more than barely good enough because the hawk will never actively like it, at the best she will put up with it, being the reasonable creature that she is. But the hood that gives her even the least discomfort is a thoroughly bad hood.

The mere fact of being prevented from seeing is the least hurt, that we do know beyond any shadow of doubt, indeed we know that the hood can induce repose. But if the hawk, on being hooded, violently jerk up her head or open her beak and roll her tongue, retch, or keep shaking her head or keep scratching the hood (not meaning a hawk that is new to the hood), then either the chinstrap is too tight, or the edges of the beak opening are cutting into the soft parts of the beak or by merely touching them are causing irritation, or the eye-pieces are too close on the eyes, or the braces are pulling the feathers under the nape.

If a hawk show any of these symptoms of discomfort it simply will not do to take the attitude "O she will get used to it!" She will not. Although wonderfully forbearing and slow to take offence in these matters, the hood if not put right, will surely create a certain barrier between herself and the falconer which will prevent that full confidence without which he can never really say that he has "got" her. A bad hood can cause actual pain which, if unheeded, will set aglow a spark of dislike which, in time, will smoulder into hatred for the unfeeling falconer, and no wonder. It does not matter much if a hawk can see a little through the beak opening, but on no account must a glimmer of light penetrate the seam of the hood over her eye, for that worries her a lot.

It has been said that "The hood is half the hawk" and that

"A hawk is as good as her hood." Such sayings rely upon exaggeration to drive home their meaning, but they do contain a powerful element of truth.

Even a good hood can become a bad one if it lose its shape which it is almost certain to do if habitually carried in one's pocket. After casting off a hawk it is far better to secure the hood by a large safety-pin, passing through the beak-opening, the safety-pin being permanently affixed to the lapel of the falconer's jacket, rather than to stuff it into the bag where the lure can crush it.

One can sometimes hear impressive examples of the falconer's voice when a tassel gentle has to be lured back again, but however clear and true it rings the voice is hardly able to cover the mile (and more) radius that a good whistle can do, on a still day. The best that I have ever come across is the referee's "Acme Thunderer," magnum size, metal whistle. Unfortunately it is difficult to get to-day. Smaller sizes are obtainable in metal and larger ones in bakelite, but they are not quite so penetrating.

A whistle is a most powerful ally when a lost hawk has to be found. Its shrilling pierces the woodlands and searches the hidden valleys, bidding far above the human voice to reach the truant's ears. In its very loudness is its only fault, for, so far-reaching is it that it often alerts those hawks left behind in the weathering enclosure and causes those, yet to be flown, to strain at the leash in their anxiety to join the distant hawking party. Even old hawks at the block, who ought to know better, get excited, and I have even seen young ones, hooded and on the fist, suddenly tighten their feathers and bate to be off at the exhilerating sound. But, well, you cannot have it every way.

HACK HUT—HACK GROUND

A HACK hut should be five or six feet high with roof sloping down from the front to the back, and its interior should be roomy enough to allow its occupants plenty of air so that they need not suffer from a midsummer's sun. The hut should face south-east and the doorway should be wide so that the young birds can receive as much of the early-morning sun as they wish. The door should be detachable, of narrow framework, and covered with wire-netting so that it obstructs as little air as possible when closed. The floor should be of turf or short heather with due provision made for drainage so that, away from the doorway anyway, it always remains perfectly dry. The inner recesses of the hut must always remain cool, if necessary the roof and sides can be covered with fir boughs to prevent their getting heated by the sun.

During early days the only furniture needed in the hut are small blocks for the nestlings to perch on. These will be removed when the young hawks are flying about outside and becoming wild, and a chair put in for the falconer's comfort so he can continue to observe them through peep holes. Thus the hack hut later becomes his hide.

As long as the young eyasses use the hut the door should be closed at night, for their safety, and opened again early in the morning. When they sit about outside, the door should be taken away, for if left open on hinges they struggle against it on the wrong side, trying to re-enter the hut or merely trying to pass through the wire-netting instead of going round it.

To prevent the youngsters from straying the hut can be enclosed with a wire-netting fence allowing them plenty of room in which to play about. The fence can be removed as soon as they can fly. This enclosure is all right if there are only one, or two, falcons of the same age, or only one, or two, tiercels of the same age to be hacked, but as a tiercel invariably flies before his sister does, and as the falconer may have several hawks of different age groups to hack for himself and other people, the wire-netting fence presents a difficulty. For when the most forward hawk begins to fly it often happens that in returning to the hack-hut enclosure it crashes into the wire-netting fence and does itself no good by feverishly trying to force its way through to the others. On the ground a young hawk at this age is very nimble and it is psychologically bad for it to have to chase it to effect capture in order to put it over on the right side of the fence. Even before it can fly properly a fledgling eyass will nearly always manage to surmount three-foot wire-netting, generally by way of the supporting posts. A six-foot fence is impracticable because by the time the eyasses can surmount it in flight they are too strong on the wing, to be safe, to take their first flight. Apart from that such a high fence is too formidable a barrier to the faltering flight of a returning young hawk which, as yet, is too inexperienced to know that she cannot fly through wire-netting.

For me, after many years of experimenting, wire-netting and other kinds of fencing round the hack hut are "out." The only satisfactory kind of boundary is a ditch or trench, in particular a ha-ha. This should be four feet wide and at least two and a half feet deep. It should be so cut that it slopes from the top of its inner edge to the base of its outer edge. It is unlikely that a fledgling hawk will get into the ditch, but if it does it will scramble up the ramp to regain its right side instead of attempting to fly up vertically to the top of the outer edge. The outer edge must at no point be higher than the inner edge, otherwise it will tempt the youngsters to try to fly across to it and may be the means of their leaving the enclosure before they ought to. Needless to add the ditch must not hold water.

The ground immediately round the hack-hut enclosure should be clear of tree stumps, fallen trees or trees with low branches. If there be any such objects they will make the young eyasses dissatisfied with their own playground because they will be continually fretting to reach them. Two-foot high blocks should be set up well inside, away from the ha-ha, and these should be seven or eight inches in diameter on top with a staple driven into the middle so that their food can be tied thereon. The blocks should be movable so that they can be put on the shady side of the hack hut during the noon-day heat. I discontinue the use of boards for tying their food onto, as soon as the eyasses are freely using the blocks, because they get fouled with mutes in no time.

A movable plank is necessary to span the ha-ha so that the falconer does not have to leap over, thereby frightening any young hawks into premature flight.

When the eyasses are all flying I substitute three-foot high blocks for the smaller ones in readiness for the not-far-distant day when hawks have to be caught up. These larger blocks are of ten-inch diameter on top to allow space for snaring. They have extra height so that a hanging, snared hawk cannot brush the ground with her wings. Tall feeding blocks are of course dispensed with if the bow-net be used for catching up. Each system has its adherents and who is to say that one is better than the other?

An ideal site for a hack hut is in the middle of a large field surrounded by trees. When a hack hawk takes her first flight she will, if everything has been previously properly managed, take perch in one of these surrounding trees from where she can keep an eye on the hut. From her perch she can see the others feeding, so that the risk of her missing a meal is cut to the minimum. It is an asset to have a pond or running stream, for bathing, within the ring fence formed by the trees. I have hacked hawks successfully on a moor where there have been stone walls within easy distance of the hut. If the hut be in the middle of a flat, open plain it would be most advisable to drive in a number of wooden posts, four or five feet high or more, at varying distances. Wherever hack takes place there must always be perching places within sight of the hut. I would not recommend hawks being hacked on a hill or table-land as in their early flights they would be likely to end up at a lower level, out of sight of the hut, and so get lost.

EYASSES—TREATMENT BEFORE HACK

EYASSES may be taken from the eyrie at any age. Even when taken at two or three days old they can be reared successfully by hand. At this very early age they should be fed from dawn to nightfall, about every two hours or as often as their crops are seen to be empty, on the liver, heart, lungs and the tender flesh of birds such as sparrows, starlings and young pigeons, etc. With their food they should begin to receive, from ten days old and onwards, finely chopped bones of birds. After a week they thrive on the flesh of young pigeons though wood pigeons are preferable, where procurable, on account of a certain amount of risk of frounce infection from the domestic birds to which downy hawks are much more susceptible than fully-grown ones. At least twice daily a certain amount of finely-chopped bones should be given with food to supply the calcium need of their growing bones. Casting too should be added.

As the youngsters grow their intake at each feed rapidly increases so that the number of meal times per day correspondingly decrease. It is a safe rule to feed only when crops are empty and never allow crops to go empty for long. At three weeks old they will need four meals during daylight hours, after that three meals, and when old enough to put out to hack an early morning and an evening feed, with twelve hours in between, is as much as they require.

With the number of feeds that take place daily during the early stages one is apt to get worried over the irregular throwing up of casting. There is no cause for anxiety really providing that the amount of feather given is not overdone and—this is most important—that a young hawk be never coaxed into taking a first mouthful if it shows the least reluctance to feed. It is also very important, from the digestive point of view, never to coax a youngster to take an extra mouthful when it shows the least sign of having had enough. It is far more profitable to throw away the last few pieces of meat than to get rid of them by forcing them down the hawk's throat. In any case, food left over is never so good as a new, freshly-killed supply for the next meal.

During early age the eyasses need close study at feeding times. After being taken from the eyrie they will take bird fat eagerly and, without doubt, a limited quantity is very necessary to them, but, look out for the first sign of revulsion, it will not be long in coming if you are feeding them on over-fat squabs, squeakers, or adult pigeons. How often have I seen a nestling look twice at a proffered piece of pigeon's neck, "parson's nose," or leg with fat skin on it, and afterwards seize with the greatest eagerness a clean red morsel of lean breast!

And cut bone—be very careful to cut it small enough and not to overdo it. Too much or too splintery bone scratches the delicate membrane of a young hawk's mouth and throat so that infection gets in, and your high hope for the hawking season goes down with frounce.

In regard to the feeding of nestlings modern falconers have come a long way since the days when the one answer to the food question was beef. In my early years I fell into the error, as did other falconers, of giving butchers' meat. Now I know why my eyasses of those days had such lustreless plumage and why their flights and tail feathers were so brittle. But they lived those hawks did, or most of them, although never—as I now realize—in full health. The eyasses that did not survive this food were the ones that were taken from the eyrie before they could stand. These succumbed to what the old falconers naively called cramp and just left it at that. Now we know that the cause of their suffering was a calcium and vitamin deficiency through incorrect food and that rickets would have been a more accurate diagnosis. What we do know for a certainty is that, other things being equal, they would have thrived on an all-bird diet. The only advice I have to give to young falconers now, in regard to the feeding of butchers' meat, is of the variety that one associates with Mr. Punch—don't.

My advice in regard to birds, as a food, is don't give the fatty-degenerated meat of old hens and old pigeons. The breast meat of chickens is not relished and it is doubtful whether such pallid stuff has the nutritional value of the darker meat.

Very young chicken is not sufficiently nutritious, neither is rabbit. Bird liver with the gall bladder removed, in the case of large livers, is excellent as a food supplement because it is a rich source of Vitamin B.

Hawks of all ages dislike bruised meat and congealed, black blood, and every effort should be made to cut out every shot-gun pellet.

Surgical tweezers is an excellent instrument to use in the hand feeding of nestlings. For cutting up meat there is nothing better than a strong pair of scissors. In cutting up the wings, legs and neck of birds cut very small pieces that are to contain the bone so that no soreness will be caused in swallowing. It is best not to give the humerus bone of the wing as, being hollow, the cut pieces often have sharp edges. And while on the subject of comfortable swallowing it does the youngsters no good to be given too many large pieces of meat, even without bone, that cause them to expend a lot of unnecessary energy in getting them down.

When the nestlings are firmly on their feet they must learn to feed themselves. This is a time of some little anxiety as they are never keen to make the effort, having become so used to the lazy habit of merely opening their mouths to receive food. The first meal of the day is the best moment to make a start because they are then at their hungriest. Tender young pigeon, that will not resist too much the nestlings' first feeble pulling, is as good as anything else for the first few lessons.

In my opinion it is not advisable to tie their food down for some time, not until they have become thoroughly used to feeding themselves. When food is tied they are denied the use of their leg muscles in feeding and it is important that these be developed. A young hawk wants to grip the meat with its toes as Nature dictates, and, naturally when it first attempts to feed itself it should not be denied this encouragement, otherwise it will get into the bad habit of merely standing astride to pull its meat. It is nearly as important for the eyass to learn to use her feet as it is for her to learn to fly. Perhaps you, reader, will allow that this may be all right provided that there be only one nestling to deal with, but you may protest that if there arc two or three they will snatch food off each other and the first seeds of carrying will be sown. My reply to that objection is yes of course they will grab and thereby they will learn to use their feet the more effectively. The desire of a young hawk to possess its own rations is inherent in it. Whether it can drag its meal away from the others or not makes no difference. You cannot root out this natural propensity. I do not advocate that, later, when the eyasses are flying at hack, their food be just thrown to them, simply because we do not want them to form the habit of flying away with food in their feet. Yet in the best regulated hack pieces of meat do get wrenched off now and again and carried. It cannot always be prevented, but there is no need for pessimism when it happens. For a hawk to carry from another is a very different matter from a hawk carrying from the falconer. It would be very foolish if one were to approach a feeding hack hawk that has a stolen piece of meat in its foot, for, being semi-wild. she would carry, and once having carried from man she would be liable to repeat the offence later on under less provocative conditions. If she begin to carry in her early days of training it is solely because something has gone wrong in the personal relationship between the falconer and his hawk. By then it may well be that the seed has been sown of a permanent, bad habit.

After five or ten minutes the nestling will get tired of pulling and it will have very little in its crop. It may try again, but after half an hour has gone by it is best to give it the rest of its meal by hand. Try again at noon and again in the evening. Three feeds a day will now sharpen its appetite for each meal, and at each meal it will show increasing strength. Gradually cut down the amount of hand feeding until you can feel assured that it can feed itself completely. After some days hand feeding will cease and by that time your pupil will show more feather than down. When that stage has been reached there is no further need to give cut bone. The young hawk will now only occasionally make her crop bulge when she feeds. Resist the temptation to fill it up with the tit-bits that she would most assuredly take if given the chance. Though her greed demands them her body does not need them because, from now on, she must rid herself of the nestling's flab and paunch.

If taken at only a few days old nestlings should be bedded

on thick warm flannel, and covered lightly with knitted wool much of the time. At night they need to be put in a warm place. But do not put them in a hot linen cupboard or over a hot-water tank and then, while getting into bed congratulate yourself on how well they are being cared for in the cheerful anticipation that they will be all right until dawn. The fact is that during the "cradle" age young hawks cannot be visited too often. So then, before you jump into bed, go along in your pyjamas and take a look. If you have only one in the basket it may he all right. If there are two or more they generate quite an amount of heat when huddled together. You will know whether they are comfortable by their breathing, if that is quickened they are too warm, but if in addition they have their mouths open they are much too hot and their woollen covering must be removed. Then watch for an improvement in their condition. If that does not come take them away and put them on a chair at your bedside. You had better read in bed until quite satisfied that they are safe for the night. It is well for the youngsters if you are a light sleeper so that you can turn on the light now and then. By putting a hand over them you can ascertain whether they are too cold.

A shallow box makes a good cradle, the air at the bottom of a deep one is apt to get stagnant, but a basket is better still as it allows the air to pass through.

When nestlings become impatient of a covering over them it is expedient to bed them on clean hay as they are then in less direct contact with their mutes. There is here, however, a danger to be guarded against, for at feeding times pieces of meat get dropped into the hay. Every single one must be picked out again so that a youngster will not find a piece, between meals, and swallow it plus the hay adhering. A few bents may not kill but more certainly will.

As every aid to health has to be enlisted, while nestlings are growing, the life-giving rays of the sun must not be denied them. They need the rising and the setting sun. The talconer, in his pyjamas if need be, must be out with the precious basket or box very early in the morning so that he can put it in the sunshine. If he still wants his bed after that he may return to it but only to doze with hawks on his mind. It may be very well for him not to visit them again until after breakfast, but his convenience does not necessarily tally with the hawks' who by then are probably gasping in the sun's glare. His charges must never be left to suffer discomfort of any kind because it puts the brake on growth. So all along the line from the cradle to the hack hut, the falconer is continually dancing attendance on those pleasantly ugly, fat, downy lumps which are so utterly dependent on him. His servitude to them is ungrudging because he knows that by giving them everything he can possibly bestow they will enter the life of a trained hawk with every advantage. Each one of those privileged youngsters he will regard as being potentially the best hawk ever and he will lavish accordingly all the care on it of which he is capable.

A day or so before nestlings take their first lesson in feeding themselves it is good for their health to dust them liberally with Lorexane which is the I.C.I.'s last word in parasiticides. The best time to do this is before they are put in the early morning's sun because the sunshine makes the parasites surface into the powder. They should receive another dusting shortly before being put into the hack hut. After they have rid themselves of surplus powder on their down they will need new bedding as a precaution against their getting powder in their lungs.

Bearing in mind the danger of their swallowing hay nestlings must be taken out of their basket from the time they begin to feed themselves and put into a movable, wire-covered pen on a lawn. Unless there has been recent rain they will take no harm on the short turf but will, in fact, demonstrate their pleasure at having firm ground under their feet after their springy bed of hay. If the grass is slightly damp their pen can be put over perfectly clean sacks. When being lifted in or out it is bad to hold them, struggling, by one hand, such useless expenditure of energy should be spared them because we want them to save all they have for growth. The proper way is to cup the two hands under each one. Anyway it is best to handle them as little as possible, so that it is all the better if they are left out in their pen during the day as the firm ground is good for their developing leg muscles and they will benefit from fresh air.

Due provision must be made, of course, for shade and they must be shielded from wind. Before successive feeds the pen should be moved to clean turf and it is nearly always possible to do this without catching hold of the nestlings. All the day long one must be watchful for a sudden shower of rain so that they can be brought in in time. Even if the weather be set fair it is best to bring them in at night where no dew can reach them and where they are safe from nocturnal prowlers.

This "lawn" treatment however only lasts for a few days because of their rapid rate of growth. By then they will have become eyasses claiming their right to be put into the hack hut.

Very probably my reader has been wondering why I have troubled myself to write about the care and treatment of downy nestlings. For him, no doubt, the question of "cradle" days does not arise for, in obedience to the time-honoured decree, he likes to take his eyasses ten minutes before they leave the eyrie. By doing this he eliminates the risk of his hawks becoming screamers, and that is a very good reason.

Those of us who have been assailed at some time or other by the abomination of screaming will want to skip any description of it, but for the benefit of any reader who has not actually experienced it it can be said that screaming is the one vice that is calculated above everything else, to make a falconer disburden himself of his patience. It is not so much the volume of noise as the detestable *quality* of it that causes us so much pain. It is so utterly miserable. It sounds like, and is probably intended to be, one vast complaint, and this is the more irritating because the screamer has nothing to complain about. It humiliates the falconer and mocks all his loving care for the debased creature that hurts his concepts of the dignity of the Peregrine Falcon. Its effect on an observer's impressions is to make of Falconry a laughing stock. Equally objectionable are the contemptible habits that go with the noise. When taken on the glove a screamer shuffles on with a horrid little creeping movement, the ends of its toes peeping from under the blowzy, puffed breast feathers. It droops its wings, loosens every feather and with narrowed, glazed eyes looks so irritatingly ill. As the miserable, distorted creature sits ungrippingly, barely balanced, on the fist anyone would think that only a puff of wind is required to blow it off.

I will forego the doubtful pleasure of describing its feeding habits, suffice it to say that a screamer can be spotted at once, during one of those rare, miraculous spells when it is not screaming, by the greasy, darkened patch of feathers on the lower, left side of its breast, caused by its mouthing its own puffed feathers while eating its food on the fist.

The long-suffering falconer, desperately seeking some little encouragement, may remind himself that this poor travesty of a hawk is in actual fact, by its very behaviour, paying him a compliment, for she is thus addressing herself to him as her parent. Had she been left to her natural parents she would be screaming and mantling and all the rest to or at them just as she is doing now to her human foster-father. No wonder the old birds drive their progeny away as soon as they decently can.

When eyasses are taken from the eyrie at the age when they are nearly ready to fly their captor is, to them, their enemy. Their instinct tells them that and their first impressions support it. Very young nestlings, not having reached the age of intelligible impressions, have only instinct to go by. Impressions come later by which time the falconer has entered their consciousness as parent. That is why they scream. Whereas the later-taken eyass, old enough not to be fooled by the human parent idea, changes its hostile attitude, through being fed by human agency, to one of friendship, but so guarded that the screaming motive has no place in its consciousness. It is true that an early-taken, screaming, human-parent fixed nestling will look up and scream at an adult hawk or anything flying over that superficially resembles one, but that is only mechanical reaction.

The suffering a falconer has to endure from a screaming hawk is a high price to pay for taking it early from the nest. It may well be asked why take it early? In my case the chief reason is that it is the eternal search for bigger and better eyasses that has tempted me to diverge from the well-beaten path of orthodox practice. As all falconers are experimenters at heart I like to think that those who read these observations

49

will not find them the less interesting if they cover subjects not usually found in books on Falconry.

You may think that the average falcon is big enough and I would agree that she is when partridge or rook is the quarry, but for grouse, black-game and wild duck (mallard) I personally want a hawk that is heavier. I want her of a weight that will make her stoop so hard that the astonishingly tough old cock grouse cannot get up again to gain the sanctuary of bracken. And I want that extra speed that goes with extra weight. From knowledge gained from experimenting along the line indicated I am now of the opinion that early-taken eyasses do tend to grow into large hawks. The theory is that they receive more food from the human hand than that which they would get from their parents, and that a larger intake of food produces a larger hawk. (As all who have studied different eyries are aware, clean-picked bones are more often found on the nesting ledge than food, and young hawks spend an appreciable portion of their day in hunger.) This is effective only when *downy* young are taken during, or before, their maximum growing period. Once they begin to feather their ultimate size is already determined and no amount of hand-feeding will make any difference.

Does the result support the theory? In seventy-five per cent cases, no. In twenty-five per cent, yes. All the largest eyasses I have had have been taken in the early, downy stage. I can only guess that the seventy-five per cent remained no more than average size because coccidiosis or capillariasis had put the brake on further growth. The heaviest of the one-in-four large eyasses have not exceeded two pounds nine ounces which is encouraging but far short of the three pound Peregrine I would like to see produced.

To estimate in terms of percentage on the result gained in regard to size is comparatively easy. I can only give a general summary as to the quality of the eyasses produced in this way, and when I say quality I mean of course their effectiveness in the Field. At the outset I must admit that the best eyass I have ever had was taken at the orthodox age, *i.e.,* when she was nearly fledged, but, leaving her out of the reckoning, all I can say is that during approximately ten years that I have been flying eyasses that were taken as downy young I have had hawks that, with some exceptions, have been surprisingly, consistently good. Lest it be judged that I am biassed in favour of an experiment that I wish so desperately to succeed I will confine my assessment to the statement that the average of these hawks was, at the very least, fully equal to the average of those taken from the eyrie when they were feathered.

So having put a fine point upon honesty I can feel free to do a certain amount of particularizing. A characteristic of these screaming hawks is their hot-temperedness which, though inconvenient to their handler, certainly does tend to make them stick most determinedly to the tails of their quarry. In other words they are courageous. It appears that, in the chase, they have their one opportunity for an outlet to their repressed excitability and irritability. They arc, compared with non-screamers, completely fearless of man, as would be expected, and it may be that this absence of fear in their character gives them an overweening confidence in their ability when flying quarry. I must add here, in parenthesis, that this refers more particularly to unhacked screamers. Many falconers consider it advantageous for eyasses to become thoroughly wild during hack. Perhaps they hold this view because they associate wildness with an absence of screaming, but a hawk at hack becomes wild because it was taken late from the nest and would not scream anyway (unless it catch the contagion from others). Wildness has no intrinsic value of its own. On the other hand tameness presents us with enormous advantages even if we do have to pay for it with split ear-drums. Let us examine these advantages. The fearlessness of very early-taken eyasses continues right through hack. They therefore do not require the noose or the bow-net at the end of it. They do not have to be caught and frightened. It is an easy matter to accustom them to the lure during hack so they can be entered to quarry within a day or two after being taken up.

A shy hawk is not a whit more effective at taking quarry just by reason of its shyness. Shyness in a hawk, in any case, is a trait that the falconer must overcome, often at the loss of valuable time. It can be an obstacle to early entering which is of vital importance, for if a hawk arrive in the field too late in the season for young and moulting quarry she has very likely "missed the bus." There are certain eyries that are characterized by the shy hawks they produce. Eyasses from some of these eyries are very good—potentially, but they cost the falconer a lot in nervous strain in overcoming this inherent wildness if they are to be entered in time. They have a nerve-racking habit of leaving the lure in a flash while he is making in. If left out for only one night they can hardly be taken up the following morning without having recourse to some form of catching aid. Yet if these hawks had been taken in the first place before commencing to feather they would have given none of this trouble. They would have lost nothing in flying performance—but they certainly would scream.

Many falconers think that the nuisance they have to suffer from the vice of screaming is too great a price to pay for any grand total of advantages. But, surely, it is worth it for a really good hawk even if there's the devil to pay. There is the type of falconer who would turn down a hawk without further thought if it screamed, but, happily there exists the other kind who would at least give it a trial to find out whether it has other component parts beside powerful vocal organs. It would appear that the former, if he thinks about it at all, errs in the belief that the hawk will continue to scream for the rest of its life, whereas the truth is it will have stopped screaming before the end of its first season if given the right treatment. I have never had one that did not and I have had many screamers.

There is one, and *only* one course to adopt to effect a cure. Fly the hawk seven days a week right through the season. If it does not soon begin to kill regularly then there is every justification to return it to the wild where nature will teach it the hard way. But if it vindicates itself as a trained hawk by flying quarry well you can put your thumbs up, for the hawk will have gained victory and so will you by your patience and tenacity of purpose. Before the end of the season, if you do your part by giving her enough flying, she will have stopped screaming and it may well be that you will have a hawk to be proud of. Her whole character will have been transformed. Before then she will have learnt that she is not, after all, dependent on the falconer who, to her awakened consciousness, has emerged from the rôle of parent to that of partner in the chase, so that the motive for her screaming no longer exists. She has grown up because she can kill for herself, and well she knows it. After such a schooling her manners, by the time she is put down to moult, will very likely be equal to the best passager or haggard. But, I repeat, such a happy state of affairs will not be gained unless she be flown every day throughout the season. It is of little or no avail if the falconer stop flying her by the end of September or October, for unless he continue towards the end of the year she is likely to carry forward her screaming into the next, though she will moderate her voice as she gets older.

HACK—ITS ADVANTAGES AND DISADVANTAGES

BETTER results will be obtained if two or more hawks are hacked together than if only one be turned out. There is some risk of an only hawk getting lost when it begins to fly. It needs others of its kind to linger round the hack hut where it could see them feeding when the next meal times comes round, for the very finest lure to induce a strayed hawk to return is the sight of another one in the act of feeding. Apart from that the screaming of others keeps it in touch with home after it has spread its sails to the breeze and gone off on its first journey into the world.

I once turned out a single tiercel to hack. It became lost after its first flight. For four days I managed to keep in touch with it, putting food down wherever it was found. This was a state of affairs that could not go on as its distance from home increased, and I anticipated that very soon contact with it would be lost completely. Fortunately, as it transpired, at that time I was keeping a young falcon of the year for a friend. As it was not destined to be hacked it was kept tied to a block on a cottage lawn, half a mile away from the hack hut. This young eyass was a powerful screamer and for once I had occasion to bless the vice because the lost tiercel, led by the screaming, found the source of it and, pleased at his discovery, came down and made friends with the falcon. I took her up and pegged her block by the hack hut where very soon he found her again. After a few days I was able to return her to the cottage by which time the tiercel had established himself properly at hack.

Another reason why cyasses should be hacked in company is the element of competition which provokes each one to fly much more than it would if alone, for a lone hack hawk usually sits about too much in quiet contemplation.

The falconer can learn much as to the respective merits of each hawk by watching them all as they fly, as they chase each other, stoop and counter-stoop. There is always one that dominates the others. Watch for the bully that will hardly let another take wing without launching into an attack on it and causing it to scream in apprehension. It is a safe bet that that one is the hawk of the year.

Hack is one of the most enjoyable phases of Falconry, for during that period the falconer can have the entertainment of watching his hawks in flight without having any immediate anxiety for them. There is a feeling of holiday in the air, both for the hawks and for the falconer who can watch them in relaxed detachment. Later in the season he is not so likely to be seen with his hands in his pockets while he watches a hawk fly.

Tea in the garden is a pleasant enough affair on a summer's

afternoon, but when there are hack hawks at liberty round the home the hour can be positively enchanting. With tea-cup in hand I have spent many enjoyable hours looking up into blue skies watching the joyful soaring of hawks at play. When they come overhead the distant tinkles of their bells can just be heard. It is possible even then to identify individuals if they wear bells of distinctive tones. Towards the end of hack I can usually identify "the pick of the bunch" simply by its bells.

The bells that are put on every eyass, before turning out to hack, should be the pair that has carefully been chosen for her to wear throughout the season. Someone in the past has recommended that extra large and weighted bells be put on to *prevent* a hack hawk's preying for itself so that it may be kept out longer. It is difficult to see just what could be gained by so thwarting a young hawk's natural progress. A hawk weighted like this would not soar, but what is the use of hack if she cannot use the opportunity to accustom herself to the upper air? After all a good hawk is a highflying one. She would not be able to catch anything, but the chief aim in hack is for the hawk to end up with a kill. And as to her being left out the longer, well the greater would be the pity, because the longer she be left out so cruelly handicapped the more demoralized she would become.

Needless to say an eyass should be kept at hack for as long as possible which usually means about a month, counting from the day that it begins to fly to the time it is taken up.

During its weeks of freedom it frequently chases most kinds of birds that it sees in the air until the day comes when it kills. A falcon flew past me one evening with a bat squeaking in her foot. Once a hawk has killed it is wise to make immediate preparations to catch her up, for all at once she becomes a creature not to be trifled with. It may be tempting to leave her out for a few more days on the principle that the more she kills the better the hawk she will be when finally tied up on the perch, but it is a fearful gamble. I once had a falcon that killed within little more than a fortnight after giving brilliant displays at flights at the local curlew. She left the hack after that kill. For ten days many hours a day were spent in the hut, with the nooses all set, in the belief that she would be sure to return just once, but she never did. During that anxious period we received reports of her being seen at ever increasing distances away. That was not the only occasion when "the hawk of the year" has got the better of me.

Sometimes an eyass comes to the falconer when it has already grown into the brancher stage. It is then quite a problem to decide what to do with it. If there are already others at hack it may be turned out with them at some risk of losing it. The falconer might be tempted to tie her to a block by the hack hut before turning her loose, hoping that by allowing her time to get used to the others and to the surrounding scene the risk of losing her will be reduced when the time comes to set her free. But there is considerable danger in tying up a young hawk, whose primaries still have some blood in them, even on thick turf, but if the ground be at all hard she is almost certain to injure her first and possibly her second pair of flight feathers. After, as a consequence, these have come out she will grow others but as it will be six weeks at least before the replacements are hard-penned her chances of successful, early entering will be reduced. At the worst these flights may grow diseased, when that happens the hawk can be written off as a dead loss because she will not allow them to grow their full length. Being diseased they irritate and so she keeps pulling them out as successive attempts at growth are made.

With all this in mind the safest course is to put the brancher in a clean, cool shed until she is hard-penned. During this waiting period much time and effort must be spent in getting on familiar terms with her. She must be coaxed into feeding on the fist with the minimum of delay so that when the time is ripe to put her outside at the block she will not be dangerously wild. If the intention be to hack her the transition from shed to hack ground can be done with such competence that she will not have been frightened. There must be no bungling otherwise the falconer will have to start all over again when he gets her outside.

After the brancher has been put out at the block by the hack hut the next step is to teach her the lure because, being by now hard-penned and so beyond the fledgling stage; it would be too risky to cut her loose without first flying her to the lure over the hack ground for a week or so in order to get her used to the locale. There is nothing to be gained by showing her the hood as one's immediate and sole aim is simply to get her on the wing with the minimum of delay. From the first day of flying her she should be left loose for gradually lengthening periods from day to day until, within a week to ten days, she can be given complete liberty. Supposing that the evening feed is at six o'clock it should be possible to put her on the wing from half-past five on about the sixth day, five o'clock on the seventh, four o'clock on the eighth, two o'clock on the ninth, and then at noon on about the tenth and last day. The hawk should not of course be stooped to the lure, as she is required to sit about in nearby trees as much as she will so that she will thus safely familiarize herself with her surroundings. If from the first she has been accustomed to the whistle at feeding time that will further greatly ensure her keeping in contact with the falconer and incidentally the hack ground, during these latter days.

Few falconers ever question the value of hack. The idea of giving eyasses their freedom so that they can fly strongly before training begins seems right and natural. It is argued that the same young hawks, had they not been taken by man, would have to gain similar flying experience before being able to kill for themselves and no one can deny that. What one is apt to overlook, however, is the fundamental difference between young hawks hacked under the tutelage of their natural parents, and those hacked, under man, with no more to guide them than blind instinct. It may be that those, under the latter category, which come out of hack with a kill to their credit are as well prepared to fulfil their natural function of preying for themselves as their wild contemporaries. But what of those that are caught up before they kill? Leave each eyass out until it does kill might be the perfect answer to that question. In theory it is attractive but not very workable in practice to be training some hawks and hacking others at the same time. Unless there is a clean finish to hack for all the hawks the period will drag out so much that it will probably conflict with the early entering to quarry of the hawk first taken up. Granted, then, that expedience demand that the first kill be the signal for all the hawks to be caught up we can return to the question—what of those that are caught up before they kill? Are they the better for having been hacked? They can at least fly strongly so they have that immediate advantage over the unhacked eyass, but there are other comparisons to make.

The unhacked eyass has never known defeat because the opportunity for it has been outside her experience. The hacked hawk has been defeated scores of times, for during her weeks of liberty she has been continually outflown and out-manœuvred by the birds she has chased several times a day. The unhacked eyass has the raw courage of inexperience. The hacked hawk may have already formed the habit of "blinking" her quarry, lacking the practical lesson and demonstration of her parents on "how it is done," lacking the parent bird's presentation to her of the quarry that she herself had just missed, that she may feed her body and sustain her courage on it.

In short the morale of the eyass that has failed to kill at hack may not be of the highest when, later, she begins to fly quarry as a trained hawk. She may start well enough but is all too quick to recognize quarry that is adroit and swift of wing. We can almost sense her thinking to herself O! I have seen that sort before! Then she turns aside on spread wings to rest on the breeze and the barometer of our hope for her falls, and we know that, as far as that particular hawk is concerned, it is unlikely to rise permanently to "set fair." For when once a hawk gives up so soon in an attack it becomes a habit much too easily and much more often than not.

On the other hand when an unhacked hawk first flies quarry it is a case of a fool rushing in. She seems determined to crash into any moving object that has a pair of wings on it. You may laugh at her clumsy effort, but you have got to give credit for her tenacity of purpose. Day after day her zest remains undiminished while quarry continue to elude her. She is, after all, only repeating what her contemporaries went through while at hack, but there is this vital difference—*they* were beyond the falconer's control, but in the case we are now dealing with the raw, unhacked eyass can be assisted in the fulfilment of her destiny, for you can pick for her the place and time for flights at quarry and so greatly increase her chance of early victory before her courage begins to flag, before she begins to *give up*. And during these days of her schooling her flabbiness is turning to brawn, her wind is improving so that she no longer returns to the lure with open mouth, her flying becomes more buoyant and her footing less clumsy. In fact she soon arrives at the stage where, in flying ability, she is the equal of the hacked eyass.

Another advantage that the unhacked eyass brings to the falconer is her inclination to fly in close circles round him during early days when he is trying to put up game for her. It is her way of putting into action her still strong desire to hang on to nurse's apron strings.

One could wish that the hacked eyass was like minded because unfortunately the tendency to rake away does so characterize her, and it is exasperating, to say the least, when game fly up just when she is flying wide, as they always do. Being comparatively experienced in flying, with a month's hack behind her, she is sufficiently blasé to fly at her own convenience which does not suit the falconer's. It is so much easier for her to fly wide instead of in tight little circles round the falconer which the unhacked eyass patiently performs because of her greater concentration on him.

A falconer named Campbell who used to hawk grouse with Peregrines in the eighteenth century, and who wrote *Treatise of Modern Falconry*, was all against hacking nestlings. He was not against hack in itself but he believed that the time to do it was *after* the eyass had been entered. It would appear that by bringing unhacked hawks to the field with their peculiar advantages, and hacking them, or giving them some measure of liberty, after killing their first head of quarry, one might reap the best from both systems. I have tried it pretty exhaustively.

It used to be my practice to turn unhacked eyasses loose round my cottage, one at a time, for a couple of hours or so of freedom before taking them out farther on to the moor to fly them at game. Without doubt they benefit from this treatment in that their flying improves more rapidly as does their wind. But the good that it does them is offset, I think, by their acquiring the fault of the hack hawk's of flying wide, if not actually raking away, when it is required to bring them to the serious business of flying at game. Physically it does them a power of good to chase birds on their own during their daily dismissals, but here again I have my doubts as to the wisdom of letting them go their own independent ways just at the time when one has the opportunity of exploiting their youthful enthusiasm and shaping it to one's own ends.

If anyone reading this thinks that he would like to try this modified form of hack may I remind him of the inflexible rule in regard to putting an end to hack, of whatever kind, once a hawk has killed for itself. To indulge her with any more of her private freedom after such an event would be to allow her to acquire the taste for hunting and killing on her own. In any case she should not be given any playtime after the beginning of September otherwise migration would be likely to take her away.

The fact that I have continued to take grouse with unhacked hawks without giving them any after-hack has led me to discontinue the practice. I believe now in keeping them strictly to business. By doing so the falconer gets earlier and, I think, generally better results. Everything considered it is my opinion that the only justification for giving a Peregrine this kind of semi-natural life is when the falconer discovers that he has not got a very good one. It may be the means of at least waking her up to her natural responsibilities.

But to give my opinion, for what it is worth, on whether it is better to hack, in the ordinary sense, or not to hack, I would venture to say that hack is indispensable for those people who can only give their hawks a limited amount of flying, for the simple reason that unhacked hawks would not have the chance to develop fully their lungs and their wings over a short season when they are flown only two or three days a week. To those falconers who can fly their hawks every day of the week throughout the season I would say that there is more to be gained by withholding hack than by giving it. However, one more statement I must add, and that is that hack is a vital necessity where hawks are flown over wooded, agricultural country, at partridge; for no other reason than that they then learn the futility of chasing wood-pigeons in such country.

EYASSES COMPARED WITH PASSAGERS AND HAGGARDS

THERE is an old saying that the worst wild hawk is a better performer than the best trained one, a saying with which most modern falconers, I believe, disagree. In my own experience there have been instances when my own eyasses have shown their superiority over wild Peregrines in combat and in the pursuit of quarry when chance encounters have put them in fierce competition. We are familiar with the old argument that because the wild hawk spends so vastly more of her life on the wing she must be better in every way than the trained one. Personally I do not doubt this when the comparison is made between wild hawks and those trained ones that, after only a couple of months of flying three or four days a week, are kept in idleness for much the greater part of the year. Obviously such hawks do not get enough flying for them to reach the limit of their potentiality. I do not know who originated the saying that too much is as good as sufficient, but I am inclined to think that it can be applied to the amount of flying that a wild hawk does. In other words such abundant measure of exercise is not necessary to produce a good hawk. I would like to continue this argument by being so bold as to opine that a wild hawk might even profit by periods of abstinence from flying if she could have them, but as she has to hunt daily for her food, often in the roughest of weather which must impose considerable wear and tear on her, she cannot except when fog forcibly grounds her.

Now take the trained hawk. On the principle that too much is as good as sufficient she does get enough rest. While the wild hawk is expending energy the trained one is conserving it, saving it for that one period in the day when she gets flown. Until the moment arrives when she is cast off the fist she is like a hound in leash. When released she is away with the zest of a slipped greyhound. The greyhound does not have to be running about a lot of the day before being sent off to catch the hare. Likewise the hawk does not require to be flown several hours daily to fit her to catch the rook or partridge, but might she not do even better if she had received more exercise ? I doubt it, for if she were not having enough a few days of inactivity would make her noticeably less efficient, whereas it is my experience that, provided she is regularly flown of course, a short spell of rest improves her. I have proved this so completely to my satisfaction that when I want my hawk to acquit herself particularly well on a certain day I do not fly her the day before. That freshens her so that she flies with new zest. After all, the object is to keep her sound in wind and a day's rest will not adversely affect that.

It has taken me nearly a lifetime of hawking to arrive at the conviction that has directed these expressions of opinion.

For years and years I erred in the belief that trained hawks would be so much better if a way could be found to give them an amount of daily exercise that would be comparable to the wild hawk's. Living as I do in the middle of my hawking moor I have been very favourably placed to experiment in the keeping of hawks in semi-liberty, and I have taken full advantage of the opportunity.

The experiment produced a lot of pleasure and I still think that hawking in its ideal, purest form is in the keeping of a hawk at liberty round the house for the greater part of the day, seeing her flying around, soaring, bathing in the stream and otherwise amusing herself until the appointed hour, that she so keenly awaits, and then to go hunting with her in company with the dogs, and afterwards to put her in the mews and see her settle down at the end of a day during which she has never bated from restricting hand nor block. But being still an earthly pleasure it must have its share of pain, and, I am sorry to say it cost me heavily in the loss of some of my best hawks. The experiment proved how delicately balanced they were between their dependence on man and their own independence.

I now know that one must keep even the very tamest of them constantly at one's elbow so to speak, for, however tame she may be, the Peregrine is never without that hidden reserve in her character which she keeps deep within her until that day when, for some cause known or unknown to the falconer, she turns away from thoughts of him and goes her own wild way instead.

To put it more robustly it can be said that in giving trained hawks a measure of liberty you are skating on very thin ice. Now I am convinced that by flying a hawk mostly seven days a week, throughout the season, she gets all the exercise necessary to bring out all the best in her. After all, the amount of flying she gets in a day's hawking is considerable. On my particular moor where the terrain is not good for hawking I generally keep a hawk up, if she knows her business, either until she has killed, which may mean several flights lasting half an hour, or until she begins to get tired through sustained effort. In either case her lungs get fully opened and when she gets put back on her block she sits contentedly, throughout the remainder of the day, in exactly the same stance as a wild Peregrine resting on a rock. She is a picture of a hawk that has had enough flying for that day.

Some falconers claim that if an eyass be flown over sufficiently long periods she can become as deadly a hawk as a passager. Such certainly has been my experience. It takes a couple of seasons or more for the eyass to equal the wild hawk's style, but, in time, she becomes almost indistinguishable from the haggard in this respect. I say "almost" because very few, if any, eyasses ever develop quite the same lightness of wing as the haggard.

When you hear a falconer echo the old cry that a passager

70

must always be superior to an eyass it is a pretty safe bet that he does not fly his hawks after October, and you will probably find his hawking days are interspersed with shooting ones, so that his hawks are not flown every day. At the first hint of winter he is off back home again so that his eyasses never become anything more than fair-weather hawks and flyers on convenient days. So it takes a passager to show him the difference between his own flight-starved hawks and a hawk that *has* had enough exercise. If only he flew his eyasses practically every day right up to the end of the season he would not need to complain over the comparison.

Campbell (to quote him again), declares that eyasses (unhacked) actually make better hawks than passagers. He openly states that, in general, eyasses are superior to haggards for game-hawking. I, for one, would not challenge such a statement, for, consider, his eyasses were flown at game right from the beginning and always kept to it. They became specialized to this flight just as greyhounds and racehorses become specialized to their forms of sport. The wild mustang, splendid animal though it is in health, wind and limb, would not equal the highly-trained horse on the race course, nor would the dingo be as skilled in catching a hare as a greyhound. The analogies are faulty but I hope they will serve to emphasise the result of specialization which is the all-important factor in the training for game-hawking of hawks under man's tutelage. From her earliest schooling days the eyass is trained to mount over the falconer's head. Flight, for her, becomes localized in the upper air over the ground on which the falconer and his dogs are moving. Whenever she sights her prey she finds herself high above it so that her method of attack always has to be the long stoop in which, through constant practise, she becomes an expert, and no wonder, because she repeats this two or three times in an afternoon, day after day, week after week, month after month. On the other hand the wild hawk as often as not hunts her prey at low level. No one doubts that she can stoop as well as the best eyass, but the latter, after a couple of seasons' endless repetition of the same, always the same, form of attack, can, and does, stoop so superbly well that the beholder is forced into the exclamation that nothing on earth could do it better. It matters not that the haggard, through her vastly more varied experience, would beat her at all other forms of flying attack while we are concerned only with game-hawking. And do not forget that in the haggard's versatility in the sphere of flight lies her weakness, for long after she has commenced to operate as a trained hawk she is much too ready to take away after other flights that offer themselves, which should remind us that a passager or haggard left out for a night is very likely to become, through unlucky chance in her loss, a poor second to the far more reliable eyass.

Having extolled the highly-trained eyass it now remains for me to write something in regard to the wild-caught North-European Peregrine, passagers and haggards. Most of them, but not all, fulfil all that can be expected of them in their performance in the field when they are trained. They are wonderful. For a substantial part of my life I would have moved heaven and earth to get one, but experience has shown that it is largely a waste of time and effort to train them.

There are of course those rare instances where individuals have been kept in man's service for a year or two and even more, but I myself have never been lucky enough, or skilful enough, to keep one for more than a single season. Were I to train one now I would cut off her jesses and bells and let her go as soon as it became evident that it was hunger, and hunger only, that made her jump to the fist and fly to the lure. Such a hawk, and they are in the majority, always has a sad eye, and I dislike it for sentimental reasons and even more for the certain knowledge that she will repay me for all my trouble by putting all her training behind her, when she finds herself free, and continuing on her own independent way as a wild bird. She may be flown for a day only, a week, a month or even more, but the first time she is flown when not particularly sharp set she will scarcely waver in her decision to go off on her own. Or if a day be windier than usual she will not trouble to fly up against it to the lure. If she be kept up a moment too long on a calm day she will rake away beyond calling. If she see a bird flying in the distance no amount of whistling and lure waving will turn her from her determined dash for the horizon. If admiring friends come to see her fly she may object to their

73

faces and clear off. I have seen it happen.

Any one of those happenings is usually the cause of a passager's or haggard's getting lost. That is the kind of passager or haggard that I have described as having the sad eye and not worth the trouble of training. There are those rare specimens of wild-caught hawks which do co-operate with man and which really do appear to find pleasure in being trained. Not only do they make surprisingly quick progress but form an attachment for the falconer as well. I had one once, a very handsome haggard falcon. She was out weathering, unhooded, within the month of being caught. What was more astonishing still was that on her first day out in the weathering enclosure she bated from the block, on sight of me, to come to me every time I appeared. I had one other that was nearly as tame but I lost her before very long when, one day, I failed to find her on her kill. Had she been an eyass she would almost certainly have been recovered, but wild-caught hawks, however tame, rarely linger within the area where they have lost contact with the falconer.

I envy those falconers who have had less disappointment with passagers and haggards than I, though I challenge anyone to claim that he is successful in the flying of Peregrines caught in northern Europe.

FOOD

WHEN the time arrives to commence training the eyass her food must be changed from the highly nutritious, fattening diet of dark-fleshed birds, such as domestic pigeons and wood-pigeons, which formerly were necessary for growth and the building up of stamina, to something lighter. It is at this stage that rabbit has its greatest usefulness. It is unfit for general diet because its nutritional value is low. Hawks fed on it continually do not manifest full health. Their feet lack colour and their plumage lacks lustre. Nevertheless it is a good corrective after the high living of early days, and because it is cooling it comes in very well during the training period of the year when the weather is often at its hottest. Rabbits are lather prone to disease so that they need to be examined with some care before being cut up for hawk food. I would remind my reader too about previous remarks about domestic pigeons in this respect.

Rabbit makes a hawk hungry so its flesh is particularly useful in the training, not only of over-bumptious eyasses, but of newly taken passagers and haggards. It certainly is not a favourite food among hawks. They often like it as a change but it does not take long for them to get sick of it. It is sufficiently unattractive to them to make it unsafe to garnish a lure with it for passagers and haggards, unless they are extremely hungry, a state in which they cannot be kept for long except at the cost of their health. One needs to keep sharply observant for the first sign of rabbit surfeit even with an eyass, or the lure will lose its attraction for her which is a sign, anyway, that her body requires different food. Some parts of a rabbit are better than others. The front legs are liked the best, then the neck and ribs. The hind legs, more especially the saddle are almost distasteful and it requires a very hungry hawk to go on eating them with any relish. Foxes seem to be in agreement with this for it is a common experience to find the hind half of the coney uneaten where Reynard has been making his meals. Rabbit flesh is made still more unattractive if the fur be mistakenly rubbed into it for casting. The best way to get such casting into a hawk is to hammer up the pads so that all fine bone is completely smashed, and the tough, stringy tendons of the hind ones should be cut. Hawks will then eat them, fur and all, without trouble. Indeed they almost seem to relish them.

After the rabbit period is over the falconer needs to find a staple food for his hawk, not that he will keep to it entirely, because a change to pigeon, partridge, pheasant, etc., occasionally is definitely beneficial, but he will want something that can be easily procured each day, something that the hawk enjoys eating, that will keep her in first-class flying condition. Pigeon is too heating. A hawk loves it of course, but feed her on too much of it and you will find she gets independent and unmanageable. In cold frosty weather she may be fed on it three times a week, but in hot weather she is better without it, otherwise she is apt to return to the lure only at her convenience instead of at yours. Wood-pigeon is better than domestic pigeon.

Butchers' meat I most certainly rule out because a hawk cannot be at the top of her form if kept to it, and besides it carries no casting and is too quickly eaten, her breath smells on it, which is a sure sign of digestive disturbance, her feet go a horribly pale colour and her feathers become lustreless and brittle, all of which ought to be sufficient warning that it is not the right food for her. For their health, and to maintain their plumage in a glossy condition, hawks must eat a certain amount of fat. But the fat on butchers' meat is not of the right kind and is positively harmful to them. Rabbit fat, such as it is, is no good either, so, for fat requirements, once again we have to turn to natural food—birds.

One day a friend, finding that he had no other food for his goshawk, went to the butcher and bought a piece of lean, tender beef. He had never fed butchers' meat to a hawk before and, since that occasion, he has declared that he never will again, because two hours after its meal it was dead with half the beef still in its crop. Probably the beef was foreign that had been frozen though there was no frost in it when given to the hawk. It might of course have been a coincidence. The

77

gos might have died from some other cause. All the same my friend does not like such coincidences and that is why he has never fed butchers' meat again.

One may read of instances where Peregrines have turned scavengers, eating the flesh of dead beasts, but that proves nothing, except that their natural prey must have been particularly scarce in the regions concerned, or that they were particularly poor types of Peregrines. It would be imprudent to conclude from such rare instances that the flesh of cattle or horses is a suitable food to keep hawks in the height of condition.

However, having little faith in the power of argument to convince, I would ask you, reader, to pass a bird-fed hawk, next time you have to leave home, to a falconer friend with the request that it be fed only on butchers' meat and rabbit during your absence. For the sake of this dietary experiment I would wish this absence to be of not less than three months. On taking over your hawk again after that lapse of time you would be shocked to see the change for the worse in its appearance.

For grown hawks I cannot recommend anything better than chicken as a day to day food. Scores of thousands of day-old cock chickens are annually killed at the hatcheries; being light breeds they are considered unsuitable for rearing for the table. These can be begged at the hatcheries, or at the most bought for ten or twenty shillings a hundred. They can be cheaply reared if given a free range as they get older. On a free range they pick up much natural food which makes them healthier and their meat more palatable to the hawks. Everything considered I find them the cheapest food for hawks.

It is not economical to commence killing them until they are twelve weeks old, because under that age the flesh is not much relished. Neither do hawks like them so much when they are full-grown, and begin to put on fat. The thick fatty skin and massive yellow fat of old fowls is distasteful and put hawks out of condition. The breast of fowls, old or young, is the part that is liked the least, for practical purposes it can be classed as rabbit.

It is best to obtain day-old cock chicks in fairly small quantities, say a dozen or two at a time, at approximately monthly intervals, so that they come on in relays for killing at the best time, otherwise you will find yourself landed with a surplus of over-grown cockerels. As they are light breeds they command a poor price as table birds, though such flesh as they do have is, of course, perfectly good for the falconer to eat, but he will not want too many of them.

No falconer will begrudge his hawk a portion of the game she kills. It is customary to allow her to have a good feed on her first kill. I would like, however, to offer a word of caution to anyone who is about to graduate from partridge hawking to grouse hawking, and that is do not gorge a hawk on grouse. The meat is very rich and appears to put a hawk right off her best efforts for the next day or two, just at the all-important time when the falconer is so desperately anxious for his new hawk to crown success with further success so as to get her confirmed as a grouse hawk. I have seen it happen time after time when the grouse-gorged hawk, after previously making a promising start, has gone all to pieces for the next few days, even after a day of little or nothing to eat following her kill. Where before she waited-on she afterwards behaved as if she had learnt nothing at all. It takes quite a few days to get her back on form again and then valuable time has been lost. So now, when a hawk kills her first grouse, I give her the head and neck of it only, after which she seems very ready to transfer to the chicken on the glove. A small portion of grouse acts as a tonic, but do not let her have too much or she will repay you with the worst type of "hangover." The effect however is much less noticeable if a hawk be left out on a grouse kill, as a night out speeds up the digestive process.

Before jointing chicken or pigeon for hawk food the intestines and crop should be removed cleanly so as to avoid tainting the flesh, both as a safeguard against possible disease and to avoid making the meat distasteful to the hawk. The crops of domestic birds are sour and offensive to hawks. On the other hand I think it is good policy to leave in the crops of wild birds, for it may well be that the heather tips, berries, green food and seeds of various kinds have some medicinal value.

A hawk's palate is extremely sensitive. One needs to remember this in the preparation of food. The table on which meat is cut up should be kept scrupulously clean. When washed down no trace of soap should be left on it to contaminate food. In fact the meat table should be treated with reverence as if it were an altar to cleanliness and health. It is good to leave it outside, with all meat removed of course, so that the rain may wash it and the sun disinfect it. Meat should never be put down on a dusty surface as the dust from sheds and outhouses is a hot-bed of bacteria. Hawks dislike food that has been mauled by human hands. Before preparing food spare a thought as to what you have been handling. If hands are sweaty or in any way dirty they ought to be washed and the soap carefully rinsed off. If you drop a piece of meat on a floor of doubtful cleanliness throw it into the refuse bucket. Always aim to give food that is in its first freshness. Meat that may be fresh enough for human consumption may very well be not fresh enough for hawks. It is at its best while still warm. It is still good when twenty-four hours old, but once the "sweet" smell has left it it is not good enough except to be cooked and eaten by the falconer. Under no circumstances should food be given with the least shadow of suspicion of taint in it for it is better that a hawk should go hungry than risk inflamed or sour crop. It is wise and profitable to be fussy in the avoidance of disease. It is indefensible to allow laxity in the cardinal rules of health to produce it.

When killing birds or mammals for hawk food be sure to drain all the blood out, as meat with the blood in is unattractive to hawks. Rabbits make better carcasses if paunched half an hour after death.

When birds that have been shot are offered the falconer it is sometimes difficult to refuse them. After wood-pigeon shoots kind friends often bring me a couple of these birds that are so relished by hawks. They are better than domestic pigeons, but all the same they put on a lot of fat in the autumn so all surplus should be removed. But I, for one, am uneasy at the thought of hawks swallowing shot. Theoretically of course the lead pellets are ejected in the casting and no harm is done. This I have proved by purposely making sure that so many have been swallowed and then checking the number returned in the casting the following morning. I did this several consecutive days on a worthless hawk and every time the correct number was returned. On one occasion I even gave shot-pellets without casting and, as would be expected, there were no pellets under the perch next morning. She had retained them and as the day wore on I felt guilty at the prospect of their passing out of the crop into the panel. That afternoon she received her meal plus casting but, on that occasion, no shot-pellets. The next morning the casting contained every one of the pellets given forty-eight hours previously when she had no casting, so I had no further need to worry on that score.

After this demonstration it seemed logical to cease worrying in the giving of shot food. However fear became active again when I heard of a friend's hawk developing an internal growth. The growth was ultimately removed and was found to contain a lead pellet. In any case lead is poisonous and one does not like the idea of its going into a hawk's crop even though it be ejected with the casting.

The amount of food to give calls for great nicety of judgment. For approximately the first month of flying at quarry the falconer may be fairly liberal with the rations because the hawk, still in the first flush of youth, can consume generous meals and yet have a lusty appetite the next day. However a very careful watch must be kept for the first sign of slackening off, otherwise the falconer will run into trouble and critical days will be wasted in restoring obedience. For the next month or two the amount of food must be accurately gauged so as to maintain a reasonably high condition commensurate with obedience. This is a danger period for the inexperienced falconer as he is apt to overlook the fact that a change to colder weather demands an increase in the rations. There must be a level of condition below which his hawk must never be allowed to slip, for if she does she may never really fully regain her former vigour. Every day her breast-bone must be felt or she should be weighed daily.

By about the end of October the eyass will be well accustomed to the curriculum of game-hawking. Each day when the falconer takes her up from the block he will sense her keen anticipation of the kind of flight that is so eminently suited to her nature. She has by now accepted this form of hunting as her *raison d'etre* and it is completely to her liking. The experienced falconer, knowing that this satisfactory state of affairs has been attained, gradually meets her over her full food requirements until she eats all that she wants most days. By then she will show him that she is no glutton for the need to gorge herself will have passed. The falconer's carefully planned regime of diet will have reached its final stage and he will have to show for it a hawk in the full possession of her health and strength.

HOODING AND MANNING

BEFORE teaching a hawk the hood it is of paramount importance to make sure that the hood is a good one. That seems a trite remark but I make no apology for it because its importance cannot be over-emphasised neither can it be repeated too often.

Assuming that the hood is a good one the young falconer must keep in mind, when he proceeds to hood, that it is not the hood itself that the hawk jibs at but the wrong presentation of it. From her point of view the hooding-act has a lot of menace in it the way some people go about it. No wonder she is scared when a hood is pushed at her head. It must be rather like a belligerent person's fist being pushed against one's face. She does not know where it is going to stop. Even when experience has taught her that no violence is intended her nerves suffer if the beginner makes dabs or shots at her head, so she bates and continues to bate until tiredness forces her submission. When that stage has been reached and she finally sits hooded, and ruffled in composure, the young falconer makes a great mistake if he thinks merely that a little contretemps has been overcome but that he got the hood on anyway. That hawk is going to dislike him and the hood if he persist in such crude methods. But as he wants her to like him very much he had better learn once and for all that hooding is not like jumping a fence—sometimes you clear it and sometimes you don't.

A falconer can be judged simply by the way he hoods. His hooding will reveal whether he is completely *en rapport* with his hawk or not. He may be clever in other respects but if he cannot hood smoothly and dexterously he still cannot be termed a good falconer because bad hooding indicates a lack of understanding of the hawk's psychology. The man who "pops" a hood on merely by sleight of hand, who tries to catch his liawk off guard, is lamentably ignorant of the proper relationship, between him and her, that governs the act of hooding.

A hawk should never be compelled but always *persuaded* to take the hood. After all, it is asking rather a lot of her to submit to the envelopment of her head. For this reason she must be cajoled into thinking that the act is of little consequence and this is best effected by putting the hood on as unobtrusively as possible. There is no need to wave it about.

To begin with the hood should never be held before her eyes as there is no point in bothering her with it before proceeding to put it on. The plume, or leather tag if an Indian type hood, should not be held between the first and second fingers just above the knuckles because this involves presenting the whole open hand to her, while the hood goes on, so that she has a much larger object to shy at than is necessary. In my opinion the base of the plume should be held between the tips of the thumb and first finger with the tips of the other fingers lightly resting on the dome of the hood to give sensitivity. Keep the hawk well in to the body with her head nearly opposite your chin, the right forearm comfortably but lightly resting against your chest. The hood is held lightly against the hawk's crop without actually touching her. The next movement is to raise your eyes from the hood to hers so as to hold her attention away from the hood. At this moment the hood is turned upside down so that the chin-strap is an inch or two below the lower mandible. Then, almost in the same movement, raise the inverted hood, make the lightest of contact between the chin-strap and the underside of her lower mandible, which will cause her to draw her head back a little, then, without pausing, repeat the same contact and turn the hood up so that in reversing it it describes exactly the right curve to land it squarely onto her head.

It will be noted that all movement is made from underneath so that at the moment the hood comes up to her eye level it is already half on, and before it does actually cross her eyes the falconer should make a little movement with his head to make her look at his eyes instead of into the on-coming hood. There must be no hesitation otherwise the falconer's nervousness is immediately communicated to his hawk. The whole operation is characterized by gentleness and quiet confidence. The skilled falconer does it with a sense of rhythm that he knows instinctively is in harmony with the working of his hawk's mind. His manipulation of the hood is of the lightest so that it is like a featherweight going over her head. His sensibility in directing it is so fine that it scarcely brushes her head as it goes on. Note that all movement is cut to the minimum, there is no preliminary brandishing of the hood, no raising of the forearm to frighten her. It is chiefly a matter of wrist-work.

It she draws her head into her shoulders at the moment the hood is going on, so that it does not go down nicely, on no account use a heavy hand to get it there. It is futile and upsetting to her to keep pushing it down forcibly. Instead, drop your whole body sharply by a sudden giving at the knees before taking the finger-tips off the hood, she will then push her head up into the hood thereby completing the operation herself. Similarly another smart "curtsey" can be dropped so that the braces may be pulled up cleanly without drawing in any of the neck feathers.

In putting on the hood the falconer has to beg his hawk's pardon in a manner of speaking. In taking it off it is cowardly and discourteous to take advantage of her hooded state by dragging it off her head unceremoniously by one brace, on the principle that because you had to seek her favour in putting the hood on you are going to stand no nonsense in taking it off. Unhooding should consist of two movements—first, open the hood at the back. This alerts her for the main part of the operation. Second, lightly grasp the base of the plume by thumb and forefinger and, with a turn of the wrist, pull the hood off cleanly and slowly enough to allow her partially unhooding herself.

If the young falconer will observe these rules for hooding and unhooding he will avoid giving his hawk offence with the one instrument that is apt to represent for her the objectionable part of training. He will thereby make of the hood and hooding both an object and an operation as inconspicuous as it is possible to make them.

The details I have given in regard to hooding are intended for a hawk that needs extreme care in this matter, either because she is not yet fully made to the hood or because, through clumsy treatment, she is on her way to becoming hood-shy. The talconer will know well enough when these foundations for perfect hooding are well and truly laid. The day will very soon come when he will notice that his hawk, on the hood's being presented, will draw the nictitating membrane over her eye. That means that she now knows all about hooding and is quite prepared for it. It is her way of saying "Go on, get on with it." The invitation must be accepted without any hesitation or fumbling for delay will try her nerves. The hood must be slipped on with the usual sureness and extreme lightness of touch for by now the young falconer will have acquired that certain rhythm necessary for the operation. In all respects she is now made to the hood and it will be found no longer necessary to take the extreme care of the earlier stages as nothing more is needed than the presentation of the hood against her crop, a slight pause for her to know what is coming to her, and then that neat-handed, unhurried but not delayed turning of the wrist that lands the hood neatly onto her head without any suspicion of pushing it on. Though the operation will become an easy one a good falconer never becomes careless about it and he will *always* bring the hood up from *underneath* and *never* fence with the hood against the hawk's head.

If hooding drill is done properly it causes no bate. In between presentations of the hood there might be a bate or two but it must always be made a rule never to allow hooding to be the cause of one. Failure in this will cause a hawk all too easily to form the habit of bating every time she sees the hood coming to her. If hooding does cause bating then it is not being done properly, something is wrong, something that is calling out for correction. I refer to the teaching of hawks the hood, being well aware that nearly always there comes an occasion later on, usually when a hawk is well accustomed to it, that she decides on a trial of her will against the falconer's in the matter of hooding. Very likely it will be after a flight when, full of high spirits, she lets you know that everything seems to be going her way. Her eye glistens with her enjoyment of life. She is excited more than usual. But need I go on? Old falconers will know what I mean. They know before they even take hold of the hood that rebellion is in store for them. And then the presentation of the hood, the flash of wings that takes her off the fist and back again in no ordinary bate. The repetition of this again and again however tactfully you address the hood to her. It looks awful. When, after all his care, it happens to the young falconer he will probably give way to despair. His hawk is spoilt he thinks. She will be from now on forever hood-shy. The danger is that she probably will be if he gets flurried and tries to end the "scene" as quickly as possible by making faster and faster passes with the hood, forgetting in his own excitement all that he has so carefully learnt. Above everything the thing to avoid is to put the hood at her the moment she regains the fist. Allow a pause, speak to her, then try again. In the end she will be hooded all right though her wings will be hard-crossed with vexation and she will be breathing fire. Continue to speak soothingly to her so as to let her know that nothing has happened as far as you are concerned, for if there is one thing a hawk appreciates in her human partner it is his unchangeableness. If, after this "scene," you are just the same person to her as you were before she will bear you no ill-will and will have taken no harm. She may do it on a second, even on a third occasion but after that there will be little likelihood of her repeating it for she will have learnt a useful lesson in humility, and ever afterwards she will respect you and show sweet reasonableness when it comes to hooding, being willing to suffer the inconvenience in return for your never-failing consideration. Such an occasion as I have described is the only time a falconer has an excuse for not putting on the hood first go. If, in the normal course he has to make two or three "shots" at it the fault lies with him and not with the hawk.

It is easier to teach a wild hawk the hood than a tame one. A wild hawk fears the falconer more than she does the hood, it is therefore possible to introduce it to her under cover of her inherent fear of man so that by the time she has become accustomed to him, in some degree, she has already accepted the hood in the knowledge that it has done her no harm. Indeed there will have been many occasions when it will have restored her from nervousness to comparative tranquillity so that her impression of it will not have been unfavourable. On the other hand the tame, unbacked eyass, unless handled with due care, can be very cheeky about the hood. Her tameness can be a real obstacle to teaching it to her because the young falconer is apt to be deceived by her familiarity into thinking that hooding her is just an extra little something that she will cheerfully accept. And of course, she will, at first, until she begins to recognize it as being something of a nuisance. Then she will dodge it quite good humouredly as if you were having a game with her. Her good humour will not last long however it her quick turnings of her head are interrupted by a hasty, impatient, heavy-handed pushing on of the hood. A few days of this sort of treatment and the seeds of hoodshyness will have been sown. It is a sad business when a once-cheerful, companionable hawk has become soured by such ill-usage which betrays such a lack of understanding of her. The fact is that all the carefulness that is lavished on the wild hawk, in the matter of hooding lessons, has to be applied to the very tame one, the only difference being that in the latter case rather more trouble is involved. In the end, however, both will take the hood equally well and both should have suffered no bating in the teaching.

In regard to the wild hawk, either passager, haggard or newly-caught hack eyass, the bird that sits hooded on the perch since capture and has not yet had her hood off, the first step in teaching her the hood should be nothing more than opening and closing it, by the braces, without taking it off. This of course follows the due amount of carriage on the fist and gentle stroking with a feather until she bears all this, and the replacing of her on the perch and taking her up again, without protest. With all this I should include of course her fearless feeding through the hood and her putting her head down for food whenever she steps onto the fist.

Open and close the hood several times until she puts up with this first lesson without hissing. Then, in the dark mews with only one candle to give no more light than is necessary to see what you are doing, half remove the hood and at once replace it. Do this a few times until she suffers the feel of it without hissing. Then, still with the chin-strap of the hood "hinged" to her throat, uncover her eyes completely for a second then, with a turn of the wrist, "roll" it back onto her head neat-handedly and without any nervous hurry yet certainly without delay.

She will not bate if it is done properly because for the moment she will be frozen to the fist by what she sees. Then at once tighten the braces of the hood and give her a few mouthfuls through it to make her understand that, despite the shock of what she has seen, life continues as before. Repeat this a few times, keeping sharply observant for the first time she turns her head away from the hood. When she does that it means that the mews interior, the lighted candle and your face, have lost the first full force of novelty. At this stage you might judge that your hawk has had enough for the first lesson so you will feed her through the hood, and, before replacing her on the perch, just open and close the hood to keep her used to the feel of the manipulation of the braces.

The next day, having carried her on the fist for an hour or so, in the fresh air, and petted her and opened and closed the hood without trying her patience too much, you will take her into the mews as before, but this time without a candle and with the door very slightly open so that she is in a modicum of daylight. As before half remove the hood, two or three times, then completely uncover her eyes and hood her up at once exactly as you did the day before, not forgetting the bite of food by way of reward. You will not be able to repeat this more than about twice before she makes the first turn of her head for by now the mews interior is beginning to get familiar to her. So take her into another shed with a streak of daylight in it so that the shock of a new scene will keep her rooted to the fist while you can repeat the performance. When she has stood enough of this open the door a little wider so that, under cover of her growing wonder, you can hood and unhood her a few more times with increasing daylight. Next day take her from room to room in the house hooding and unhooding her, but still never keeping her bare-headed for more than a second or two. Repeat the same evening in the glare of electric light. You can do it in front of people if they will promise not to leap suddenly out of their chairs and so spoil everything by making her bate, because if she does bate it will not be so easy to put the hood on her again and that would be a very serious set-back. Next day you will be able to hood and unhood her outside in broad daylight if you have sufficient confidence in yourself, but be very, very careful not to let her bate otherwise real harm will have been done. This is the final phase of this particular lesson but it is best omitted unless you can be certain of carrying it off successfully.

Until now you have done no more than uncover her eyes momentarily and restore the hood to its original position, just to accustom her to the feel of it and to give her the impression that its going on puts an end to her fears. The importance of that grounding cannot be over-estimated and, if my reader is a beginner, he will have benefited as much as his hawk in this first lesson and acquired the necessary degree of confidence for further progress. He will do well to remember that hooding proper is closely related to that which he has already performed, in that the minimum of hand movement is essential for its successful achievement.

The hawk is now ready for proper hooding lessons. She is also ready for manning in the unhooded state. The two are complementary to each other. Where shall we carry out this supremely important phase of the hawk's training? Not in the mews because she will keep bating to try to get onto the perch. Not in a room in the house because she will bate towards the window and even with the curtain drawn she will still bate towards pieces of furniture. The stable or garage is too large because in either of them she will bate to escape you. The only suitable place for the session is a small completely unfurnished shed in which the amount of light can be controlled. The floor space should be approximately eight by six feet, not more, and the ceiling should be well clear of your head. Not even a chair is allowed for you will man the hawk on your feet. The shed must be cool for a nervous hawk soon gets her mouth open if it is warm. The reason for being so closely hemmed in by four walls is the avoidance of unnecessary bating, for the hawk will realize that in such close confinement she cannot fly away and she will see nothing whatever within the four walls to attempt to fly onto.

Darken the shed interior and commence by half unhooding and hooding her up exactly as before. Do this about twice then remove the hood completely and hold it to your side. Keep perfectly still and avert your eyes while she stares you full in the face. Do not look at her again until she bates, and that may be quite a time. It will be an unreasoning bate prompted by sheer nervousness. When she regains the fist watch her out of the corner of your eye. When she turns her head and is contemplating another bate turn your body ever so smoothly but not too slowly, with your left elbow held into your side, fist well up so that her eyes are about on a level with yours, and as often as she looks like bating again keep turning. Thus with the walls seemingly revolving round her the bating impulse is reduced because she is too bewildered by the tiny, moving, almost dark world she finds herself in with no solid object in it and no horizon. You will quickly know the right speed to keep turning to put bating out of her mind. When a bate is being contemplated speed up the turning. All the time remember to keep your fist well up because, as a general principle, a hawk held high is always less likely to bate than a hawk held with the forearm at a right angle to the body—a position in which she should never be carried.

I am not asking you to make yourself giddy by turning on your heel all the time because you can very smoothly change your turning into a gentle, rhythmic pacing up and down. Imagine you are pacing the deck of a ship. At every turn at the end you are confronted by the short length of deck in front of you which your feet will traverse as if motivated by a will of their own. With your feet taking you up and down like this you will induce a torm of self-mesmerism (which will require a certain amount of effort to stop) and that is exactly what is required. After a few bates it will be found that the hawk, too, has become mesmerised and when she has reached this state she will not bate again, not for as long as you go on, and that will be for an hour or more. The few bates that she has had at the beginning of the session were manning bates, they were not bates at the hood—that is the important thing. They will have done her no harm nor caused any offence.

All this time the hood has been held out of her sight. When she has become mesmerised is the time to start using it, certainly not before.

Begin by raising the hood to her crop while, like Felix the cat, you keep on walking. No more than that. It is best to begin making this movement while turning at the ends of the shed or cabin. Keep putting it up to her crop and taking it down again, putting it up and taking it down as you pace up and down. Do this about fifty times until your right forearm almost takes on the rhythm of a pendulum. After she has become so used to this movement that she ignores it completely take matters a stage further by raising the hood until its chin-strap contacts her throat with a feather-weight touch. Thus, while walking, you will now keep your right elbow comfortably into your chest so that the hood is carried opposite her crop without, of course, actually touching it. The hood plume is held by your fingers so that the hood is carried upside down, so that when it is raised the chin-strap is in the right position for contacting the underside of her lower mandible, continue doing this until she has become thoroughly used to it after which you can develop this chin exercise by half rolling the hood onto her head, reversing the movement just before the hood covers her eyes.

As she has already become accustomed on previous days to having the hood half-drawn off her head, and then replaced, you have at this juncture arrived at the meeting of that exercise with that which you are now performing, consequently she will not now oppose the complete putting on of the hood especially while she is in her present state of trance. So, lightly and gently, you will now proceed to hood and unhood her and, as she has behaved so patiently and well, you will not bother her with tightening and loosening the braces except only occasionally. When the hood goes on do not be always in a hurry to take it off, but sometimes leave it on for a couple of minutes or so; sometimes replace it immediately and sometimes delay it. As you now pace up and down, hooding and unhooding her, you can tell yourself that you have "got" her. The foundation for her successful hooding from now on has been well and truly laid. Hood and unhood her about thirty times, then tighten up the braces and step out into the fresh air, sit down and make yourself comfortable and let her feed through the hood.

To recapitulate on this lesson as if you had been doing it "by numbers" it can be summarized as follows:—

1. Raise hood to crop and lower it again.

2. Raise hood from crop to throat and lower it again.

3. Put hood half on and lower it again.

4. Hood and unhood.

It cannot be repeated too often that all this raising and lowering of the hood is done below the level of her eyes and directly underneath them as movement under a hawk bothers her far less than movement at her eye level. In (1) you get her used to the approach of the hand with the hood in it. (2) you develop this movement. (3) you get her used to the invitation of hooding. (4) you consummate it. Thus the whole act of hooding is taught the hawk in easy stages. If it is carried out all in one, first go, it is not surprising that the operation, so utterly alien to her experience, should be so fraught with fear for her. Whereas if she be taught hooding as indicated it will not distress her because of your tactful introduction of it. You will have persuaded instead of coerced her into its use and that makes the whole difference between success and failure.

Having by now impressed on your hawk that she has nothing to fear from the act of hooding, and having got in the preliminaries of manning, the next stage is to induce her to associate hooding with something pleasant, and that for her just now means food. This association will not remain with her for the rest of her life but the need for it will have passed by the time she cheerfully accepts hooding as a peculiar whim of her human friend, as all hawks do after they have been led into it with patience and gentleness.

So again retire into your bare little cabin on the next day with your hawk and have available some prepared titbits of red, lean meat and surgical forceps or tweezers. Allow the same small amount of light inside as on the previous day. Draw the braces and, standing still, slip the hood off and on two or three times just to make her hood conscious. Then remove it and place a titbit on its chin-strap. Holding the plume underneath with the hood uppermost, like a cup, bring it up to her and allow her to take the titbit off the hood. If she appear restive on no account persist in trying to get her to take the titbit, instead take the hood away from her, the golden rule being that the presentation of the hood and a bate must never go together for we don't want her to form that kind of association. So, if she looks like bating, raise her on your glove and do a few turns in order that her bewilderment may prevent it. If necessary walk up and down a dozen or twenty times until she gets into the same state of trance as she did on the previous day. While walking put her through the same hooding exercises as already described by numbers 1, 2, 3, and 4. It will not be long before she will take the titbit off the hood bare-headed, but, if she is the kind of hawk that will not, put the hood on (don't draw up the braces) and the moment it is on hold a titbit at the end of her beak with the tweezers. With the hood open at the back she will just be able to see the titbit through the beak opening, particularly as it stands out neatly at the end of the tweezers instead of being confused in the fingers, and of course you will aid her further by holding her in a ray of light. If she will thus take a titbit through the hood every time, the moment it is put on, that is good. If she take one before and after the hood goes on that is still further progress. She will do the latter all right after some more manning.

And so it will not be long before you and your hawk will fall into the rhythm of this exercise. Soon she will lean forward when she sees the hood coming, thinking ah! here comes a titbit! and when the hood goes on she will be poking her head forward for another one. Thus the stage of Pleasant Association with the Hood will have been reached. At the end of the session she will have quite a bit of food in her crop. Hood her up and let her finish the meal (no more titbits) through the hood.

These sessions should be held in the morning after which she will be put back on the perch and left in peace to digest her food. By the evening, when she has put over her crop, you will continue carrying her about hooded on the fist as she must not be left alone too much. Then you will sit in the house and in artificial light, and with company around, you will be quietly hooding and unhooding her (no titbits this time) but not so much as to plague her with it. Never allow her alarm to grow at anything she sees before the merciful curtain of the hood comes over her head to shut out her fears. If she once bate during these evenings of carrying you must blame yourself for mistiming the putting on of the hood. She is still a long way off the stage when she will sit peaceably bare-headed in a room with daylight coming through the windows. That will try even a tame hawk until she gets accustomed to it.

Next morning let just a little more light into the cabin, afterwards, as a preliminary, hood and unhood three or four times and reward with titbits. Then hold in your glove a piece of meat, her meal for the day. As she still has to be left hooded on the perch at nights it must contain no casting and it must be fairly easy to eat because she is going to have her first meal bareheaded, so you must allow for a certain amount of nervousness and a nervous hawk will not want to wrestle with difficult bones. When you have unhooded her don't talk to her and keep perfectly still. Perfect stillness on your part is a *sine qua non* otherwise you will only add to her nervousness. Can you stand without the slightest movement for half an hour or an hour ? If you are to be any good as a falconer you *must* be able to do this, for human fidgets just at this stage are an abomination to a nervous hawk. Quite possibly she may begin to feed within the first live minutes, but just as likely she may sit, as if carved in stone, and stare and stare and stare at you, but you most certainly will not stare back. If she sit without movement for an hour give thanks that she is having the best kind of carrying and manning. If she becomes restive, as indicated by much turning of the head, do not attempt to hood her because, with her in that state of mind, it would precipitate a bate. Elevate your gloved fist until her eyes are above the level of your head, then begin turning her, as prescribed before, and gently resume the pacing up and down of previous days, repeating the hood drill with titbits.

But, much more likely than not, she will begin to feed, probably after putting her head down many times and quickly raising it again, wondering if you can be trusted to do her no violence while she addresses herself to the food. As she sees only the same face with your eyes half closed, apparently on the edge of sleep, she renews her coinage. First she may take only tiny mouthfuls but her confidence grows and soon she is eating well. On encountering any difficulty, however, in getting meat off the bones, she stops feeding.

After her feed she will resume her staring at you. You will continue to stand absolutely still for just as long as she will sit quietly. No one will come hammering on the door to put a rough end to everything, because you will have told them in the house that you may not be in to luncheon and that you must not be disturbed unless the house is on fire. Quite often after the first feed without the hood a hawk will sit for half an hour with the brightness of fear gone out of her eye. She may rouse, she may even look quite friendly, and you sense that she is beginning to feel pleased with herself and you will look back over the brief time since you took her training in hand

and realize, with pardonable pride, that through your infinite tact and patience you have successfully steered her round all the pitfalls that lie in wait for the falconer with a newly-caught hawk to reclaim. When she begins turning her head elevate her on the glove, a little more walking until you sense that she has been steered back into tranquillity, elevate the hood to her crop, stop walking, and while she stares questioningly at you, gently slip the hood over her head and, after drawing up the braces, for the first time you can speak quietly to her again, thanking her for her co-operation. You are now well on the high road to her training.

Next morning let more light into the cabin. This time you can give yourself the luxury of a camp chair placed against the end wall so that, if it become necessary, you are still left with a little space for turning around in and walking. You can support your forearm and fist, with the hawk on it, on the arm of the chair. Induce her to pull at the meat through the hood and, after a few mouthfuls, unhood her, talking quietly to her before and after the unhooding. Before she has eaten all her ration hood her and let her finish the meal through the hood, this being the general practice, the idea being that the hood must not be associated in the hawk's mind with the end of a meal. Later on when she fully understands her rôle as a trained hawk and it is possible to let her have pretty well as much as she can eat, the hooding is best done after the conclusion of her meal, but those days are a long way ahead yet. If for any reason she becomes restive while bareheaded do not forget to raise her on the fist first before getting up out of the chair, so that all your movement takes place underneath her. To raise yourself first would be certain to make her bate.

We have now reached the stage when hooding lessons should no longer be necessary. Once the hawk is well accustomed to the act of hooding more harm than good would result from endless repetition. Until now you have taken advantage of her wildness to teach her hooding while she fears it less than she does you. From now on your aim should be to get her tame as quickly as possible. From day to day she will be fed in new surroundings with ever increasing light until she feeds fearlessly on the fist outside in broad daylight. Sometimes a recently reclaimed hawk shows fear of hooding outside in the open for the first day or two. When this happens do not try to get the hood on quickly so as to forestall a bate because you will only precipitate one. In fact *never*, on any occasion, hurry the hooding. Any departure from the deliberate calmness of this act will only make her take a fresh view of it and that an unfavourable one. So, as she is by now well accustomed to your walking about with her on the fist, take her into the mews which, with this contingency in your mind, should be close at hand. If she bate on the way at least she will not have bated at the hood, and if you allow her to bate at the hood, particularly at this stage, it can only too easily become a habit. With a roof over her head and your back blocking the light in the doorway you will be able to hood her with the usual case.

Having dealt with the wild hawk in regard to teaching it hooding, how will the very tame, unhacked eyass be treated in this respect ? Simply through pleasant association and familiarity. In regard to the former this means the frequent giving of titbits on the hood itself with one or two given immediately after it has been put on. And in between it is good frequently to put the hood up to her chin and frequently to half hood her so that for every complete hooding she gets half a dozen sham ones so that she never really knows when it is going on. This comes under "familiarity" but add to that the continual keeping of the hood before her while she feeds so that it almost gets in her way, it is then within a few inches of being on her head. For a long time, until you are certain she is *au fait* with the hood, never put it on without immediately afterwards letting her pull at a bit of tiring through it. All this is the right kind of familiarity, the wrong kind is the push-it-on-and-stand-no-nonsense treatment in the belief that just because she is tame she can be badgered into it. No hawk will ever be successfully hooded through forcible compulsion.

The most difficult hawk for teaching hooding is of course the one that is already hoodshy, either from bad hooding or from wearing a hood that hurts her or both. She differs from the others in that it is the hood itself which frightens her. But she can be got over her aversion to it with patience and time. First of all of course get a comfortable hood for her, then begin by placing it on the far end of the perch in the mews and imperceptibly advancing towards it while she feeds on the fist until her head is within a few inches of it. After a few days of this treatment the next stage is to conceal it partially in the right hand against the meat. With each successive feed a little more of it can be exposed until finally the whole thing stands out against the meat. After that it can be moved about a bit but *not* towards her. For the next few days persuade her to take titbits off it, causing her to put her head down for them. All ways and at all times watch her very closely and if she hiss at it or, worse still, puts her head up and glance wildly about don't show it to her again in the hand that day but put it back on the perch where she will fear it less. But assuming that progress has so fat been smooth the next stage is to begin advancing the hood from the meat to her with of course a juicy titbit on it. This is the first actual step towards hooding her but that operation is still a long way off yet. Then for the next few days let her meal consist entirely of titbits. Have a piece of tiring in the fist, for the first day or two, just to make sure of holding her attention away from the hood. Next day dispense with the tiring. And then when, for the first time the hood comes up to her (with a titbit on it) with her standing at attention, that will be the first real test of your progress. If she gasp at its approach immediately stay your right hand. She may recover and stretch her head down for the hood garnished with the titbit. If she does, don't meet her with it so fast that she will take fresh alarm at its renewed approach, nor so slowly as to give her time to awake suspicion. An experienced falconer would know exactly the right timing. After a few days of this treatment, after she will stand to attention on the fist without a piece of tiring and eagerly await the hood's approach, stretching out her head to receive each titbit on it, you may be sure that she is well on her way to losing her fear of it. The next step is to put the hood up to her chin with and without a titbit on it alternatively, then progressively increase the number of times the hood is thus presented to her without a titbit.

When this stage has been reached it is advisable to begin proper hooding lessons within the four walls of the cabin as already described. Put her through the exercises 1, 2, 3, and 4, as previously described a few pages back, exactly as recommended for teaching hooding to a wild hawk, always reverting to the giving of titbits on the hood every time she shows mistrust of it.

By following out this method of cure, step by step, a hood-shy hawk can be reclaimed to the hood, but remember that it will only require an occasion or two of clumsy hooding, or the putting on of a hood that hurts her, to put her back into her former acute dislike of it. So, with her, you will have to be extra careful for ever afterwards.

TAMING

MANNING and taming are two distinct developments of a hawk's training. The former is the means whereby the falconer neutralizes her basic fear of him. The latter is the creation of an alliance wherein she learns to like him. I want to stress that the former must be as persuasive as the latter lest any beginner have the mistaken notion that manning a hawk is simply a matter of carrying it, and every successive bate is nothing more than the outward sign of her "rebellious" spirit being broken down. However and wherever he might have formed this impression it is an utterly false one.

It is well to remind ourselves that bating from the fist, at its best, is a hawk's attempt to fly away from the falconer through restlessness, at its worst through fear of him or some other fearsome living thing or object near him. Whatever the cause bating is bad because it only serves to emphasise in the hawk's mind the association of restriction with the falconer's presence. To coin a rough epigram it could be said that the hand that precipitates avoidable bates is the stumbling-block to a hawk's faith in the falconer. A good falconer manages his hawk with the minimum of bates, in fact the absence or fewness of them is the measure of his degree of skill. It has been my privilege to watch experienced falconers handle their hawks throughout the day with never, a bate to mar their proceedings.

When manning is successfully concluded and taming begins it is food that plays the all-important part in the proceedings. At this stage the falconer is at his most bearable in his hawk's estimation while he is feeding her on his fist, so of course he prolongs the feed for as long as he possibly can by giving the wings and bony parts of a carcase and leaving the hawk to do the depluming. And, following the usual practice, he will hood his hawk before she has quite finished her meal, allowing her to continue feeding in the hood. The hooding should be done so smoothly that it scarcely interrupts her feeding.

Personally I do not advocate leaving a hawk hooded for hours on end after she is made to the hood. It does not make her like it any more and I, for one, do not enjoy the sight of her scratching at it every five minutes. After all the use of a hood is somewhat similar to that of blinkers for a horse— to protect her from seeing things that may frighten her, or, in other words, to prevent her bating. We cannot dispense with the hood but at least we need not inflict a hawk unduly with it when she has become steady enough to sit reasonably contented without it.

The early days of taming can be said to occur at the same time that the hawk is being persuaded to weather without the hood. And as prolonged feeding on the fist out of doors starts the taming process, the hour chosen for it should conclude the hawk's spell of weathering bare-headed which, for the first day, will be only about half-an-hour. The reason for feeding her daily at the conclusion of her weathering is that she will come from the block to the fist with the least trouble when she is very hungry and due to be fed. And her meal, prolonged as much as possible in the evening sun on the falconer's fist will finish the day contentedly foi her. It is advisable to feed her at the evening hour so that she can be put in the mews afterwards for the night where no disturbance can mar the day's good impressions. If fed earlier in the day and put back on the block she would have to be left hooded, and if by unlucky chance she happened to get the hood off it would be difficult if not impossible to take her into the mews without some unfortunate bating. As the days go by she becomes accustomed to weathering for increasingly long periods so the stage is finally reached when she is put out first thing in the morning and left to weather all day unhooded until taken up for her feed and put into the mews for the night. All this refers to the early days of taming. Later on it does not matter what hour of the day she is fed because she will be tame enough to come to the fist from the block for a piece of tiring at the end of the day.

The giving of titbits coaxes a hawk into familiarity with the falconer quicker and more effectively than anything else. It is quite remarkable how all hawks respond to them. Perhaps they evoke memories of being fed by the parent bird with which the falconer becomes flatteringly associated, or, more prosaically, they are liked because they are so easily eaten, though I am sure that the latter is not the whole explanation. While the hawk is feeding slip her a titbit occasionally. Note how soon she becomes continually on the watch for them. A wild-caught hawk or an eyass that was wild when caught from hack takes them daintily and gratefully. A haggard or passager is particularly careful not to pinch the finger that proffers them, but an unhacked eyass snatches them ill-manneredly with rough reproach at your keeping them back, biting the finger at the same time through sheet greed. The remedy is not to give her any except on the hood, when teaching her the hood, because there is no need to woo *her* as she is already aggressively tame.

To get a hawk used to your approach—that is the essence of taming, for in that moment she has to decide whether you are to be trusted. It is only when you can go and take her up from perch or block without a bate that she begins to get tame. For a considerable time after that she will continue to be on her guard when you are with her, any unaccustomed move on your part being sufficient to make her flash off the fist.

When, during early days a hawk is put outside on her block bareheaded she is conscious of two things, the first is the invitation to freedom and the second is the falconer. If the falconer walk away and leave her she has only freedom to heed and that is the wrong companion for her at this stage. So you must remain with her and keep her attention on you as much as you can. Keeping a hawk company while she is weathering is as exacting as any other aspect of taming. It is not sufficient just to be somewhere near her. It is good to sit in a chair and watch her, up to a point, but as soon as she has decided that you are just a harmless fixture she will begin to pay attention to the beckoning hand of freedom in the breeze and the moving clouds. So when you see the nervous up-thrust of her head and the loosening of her wings it is the signal to get on to your feet again so as to divert her attention from the vault of heaven to yourself, her poor slave that creepeth upon the earth. Start walking in circles round the block but never so close as to make her bate. There will be bates of course, but so long as you are not the cause of them no harm will be done. Before very long you will find yourself walking in closer circles to her. Now is the time to exhibit a piece of meat in your hand without coming to a halt. If she regard it attentively edge in closer to the block, remembering never to approach it directly. Watch her out of the corner of your eye, keeping your gaze meekly to the ground. At the same time lower your hand with the meat in it and, coming to a halt without any suggestion of abruptness, judge the moment to present the meat. If you do this to her at the level of her head she will probably take fright and bate, the psychology of a hawk being such that she fears the human hand less under her than at a higher level. So the offering should be made to her feet or just above them. If she lower her head to it do not keep her waiting or her nervousness will persuade her to give the whole thing up. But by now you will know your hawk sufficiently well to judge the exact moment to let her have it. Actually you do not want her to have the whole piece of meat because it is not intended to give her anything like a meal, it serves only to engage her attention. The titbit that you have for her is at your fingers' ends and that she takes because it is the nearest to her. Under cover of her swallowing it take your hand away well beneath her and walk away again. So you approach, you reward her for her confidence in you and pass on. After repeating this a few times she will begin to regard your retreating figure with unmistakeable regret. By then you can dispense with the large piece of meat and use only titbits which she will begin to expect every time you go near her. Always remember during the stages of taming in the weathering ground never to approach the block directly, but always indirectly, as if you were going to walk past it.

The day will very soon come when your hawk will look towards you eagerly on your entering the weathering ground. When this happy state of affairs has been reached she may be left to herself to weather for increasingly long intervals. Very soon she learns the measure of her leash and her bates become not so much the efforts of a prisoner trying to escape as an exercise to relieve pent-up energy, a form of dissatisfaction that you will soon be able to put right because by now she is ready to be acquainted with the lure. After that your pupil will be allowed to expend her energy flying in the free air.

In these observations on manning and taming I have tried to convey the overriding importance of unhurried, rhythmic movement on the falconer's part at all times. His walking keeps the hawk's attention turned in towards him. If he remain still she will look past him and will centre her attention only on freedom, and of course he does not want her to contemplate the allurement of what, during that time, is his great opponent.

So much depends on the falconer's skill in manning, hooding and taming his hawk that he can be said to be a craftsman who by the exercise of his art determines the degree of excellence his hawk, as an instrument of the chase, shall be. True, no amount of manning and taming, however well done, will make a bad hawk into a good one, but a potentially good hawk can easily be spoilt by rough and ready attempts at manning, hooding and taming. In these three phases of training especially the falconer has need to address himself to his task with all the unflagging attention of a lion tamer taming his lion. Only there is this difference, that whereas the falconer must win his hawk's confidence, I rather suspect that the lion tamer must brace himself to get confidence in his lion.

When does the process of taming end? Not for a long time. Even after a hawk is flying free every day the falconer must exercise continual care and take every opportunity to impress on her in every way that he is her friend, especially when the unexpected happens as it so often does. He must always guard against giving her any offence because she never forgets an ill-considered or hasty action on his part. A hawk cannot be said to be tame until she allow you to walk up behind her on the block without her turning round, because in turning to face you she betrays her lack of confidence in your intentions. If she preens on the block and continues to preen without bothering to turn to face you, while you walk up and stand behind her, then she is really tame.

Certain signs may be looked for in confirmation of a hawk's growing attachment to her human friend. She will turn her head upside down, saucily, at his approach. When fed at the block, during the moult, she often leaves some food over, and, on seeing him coming, jumps down and begins to feed again, obviously as an invitation for him to take her up and feed her on the fist. An affectionate hawk, although not hungry, will often show her pleasure at the falconer's presence by making pretence of feeding when he proffers food in his fist. When he puts her on the perch in the mews she steps forward onto it with deliberation. She does not jump to the extremity of her jesses. And after a hawk has become tame she must be kept tame. If you have never approached her at the double you cannot run up to her one day when you are in a hurry to catch a train. If you are accustomed to wearing a sports-coat and grey flannel trousers in her presence you cannot take her up from the block in dazzling white flannels just before going to a tennis party.

On the subject of clothes you can get your hawk used to your wearing different ones if the changes of colour, at first, are not too violent. It is convenient to be able to handle her in whatever you stand up in and she will suffer this in time. All the same she is so very much a creature of habit herself that she does not approve of changes in others, so, if you really want to make yourself as agreeable as possible to her you will respect this foible of hers as much as any other.

A creature of habit a hawk certainly is. She likes to occupy the same place on the perch every night. She likes to hear your approaching footsteps, when you go to take her out in the morning, simply because she is more accustomed to them than those of any other person. She likes to be taken off the perch in the same, unhurried way, to be hooded with unvarying timing. If you go to take her up from the block and, through some personal preoccupation or agitation, your approach differ in the least from its usual easy manner she is instantly aware of it, and her eye will search you questioningly. She likes your voice and will brighten to it as you call out to her, showing no response at all to the voices of other people, except possibly nervousness. And she likes the same old sports-coat you wear. When it becomes old and tattered and torn—well, that is a modification that she will cheerfully allow you. The more the family refuse to have anything to do with it the better she will like it and the more it will draw you and her together. Even though, every time you put it on to go to your hawk, your wife's sorrowful mien betray her heart's misgivings, my advice to you is, as one falconer to another, go on wearing it.

This conservatism in a hawk naturally leads her to prefer one master. If she be handled and flown by more than one person she will suffer from the attentions of the least competent, and may develop vices that otherwise never would have appeared.

Training is a matter of weeks, but taming is more a matter of years. In a sense a hawk cannot be said to be fully trained until she is really tame.

Occasionally one meets the type of hawk that persistently refuses to make friends with the falconer. If she keep her distance through an ungenerous nature one can do nothing except to continue to treat her with the greatest patience and deference in the hope that kindness will win her in the end. It rarely does. On the other hand there is the high-mettled type, often brilliant in the field, that shuns familiarity with man simply through the nervousness that marks the thoroughbred. That type can be won over and ultimately can become very tame and trusting. With her it is just physical contact with the falconer that is feared. In the past I have noticed that when such a hawk is held in the human hands it actually tends to break down her nervousness of the falconer instead of increasing it as one would expect. I have never deliberately man-handled a Peregrine as an act of policy, but have noticed that when this nervous type is held for imping and coping an improvement is discernible afterwards, particularly if the operation has to be repeated over a tew days.

A wild tiercel that had been caught in a trap was sent to me some years ago. Because of the injury to his feet I had to hold him in my hands a lot, from the first day, so that I could massage his feet and rub a healing ointment into them. He was as wild as could be when he arrived, but after a very few days of this frequent handling he became wonderfully tame. He would lie in my hand without resistance, eagerly stretching his head forward for the titbits on which he was fed.

I think one explanation is that after being held in man's hands it dawns in a hawk's mind that, although the creature that she fears most apparently did his worst, no harm befell her. Thus she passes the apex of her fear of him. And I think that another explanation is to be found in the mind of the man. When he approaches to take a shy hawk onto his fist, in the ordinary way, sensing her nervousness he himself becomes nervous of her nervousness but in this mutual fear he can control his physical reaction but she cannot. But when he holds her bodily in his hands his fear vanishes, for it is pushed out of his mind by solicitude for the job on hand, and by the fact that there cannot be any bating to make him nervously apprehensive.

There is no doubt that a falconer's nervousness is unfailingly communicated to. his hawk. If he can disburden himself of it and replace it with quiet confidence her favourable response is immediate. It is difficult to know to what extent this truth can operate, but that it does work is evident by the fact that some people have what is popularly judged to be a miraculous gift in overcoming the fear of wild creatures, even of those they have not seen before.

When a falconer takes on a new hawk a gulf of feat lies between her and him. The hawk will come half way to meet him over it, but, whether he consciously recognize it or not, he has to advance also from his side, on the phychological plane, in the breaking down of his nervous apprehension to her fear. In a sense it is like a progressive disarmament, on both sides, of any emotion that opposes mutual confidence. In proportion to his understanding of this the falconer is able to profit by it.

I cannot agree with the opinion occasionally expressed that a hawk can become too tame, if by that it is meant that there can be too much familiarity between a falconer and his hawk. Personally I am never satisfied until my hawk loses every trace of fear of me, and nothing has ever happened to make me regret this policy.

But if "too tame" means the undesirability of having a hawk equally fearless with strangers then I am inclined to agree that it is a form of tameness that can be carried too far.

It can be very convenient of course when a total stranger can handle your hawk with the same ease as you yourself can. It is very pretty when another man's hawk flies to your fist without hesitation. It is taming to the last degree and is very impressive, and it reflects the greatest taming ability in the falconer. But one must remember that such perfection is not an end in itself. To be practical the falconer must ask the question "Will such tameness add a single head of quarry to my score book?" The answer to that is yes it will if you are going to allow other people to fly your hawk during times that you cannot, but many falconers are not willing for others to fly their hawks and perhaps they are right.

It could be argued that when a hawk allows anyone to take it up off a kill there may well be occasions when not only another head of quarry is so added to the score book but the hawk herself may thus be saved from being lost. That argument is so good that if the matter ended there the case for the policy of having hawks equally tame with everybody would be overwhelming. But unfortunately falconers are a very small minority and there are many people who, through ignorance or malice, arc hostile to hawks. What, if, instead of a falconer approach your hawk on her kill, some unknown person, possibly with a stick, advance on her? Would you at that moment be glad for her to remain imperturbably depluming her victim, or would you wish her to fly away for fear of him before the stranger's intentions could be revealed?

Hawks that have been led to trust all mankind have occasionally met their death when that trust has been betrayed through the violence of strangers. Others that were less unlucky have been captured and thrust into rabbit hutches to languish sometimes for days.

"Equal tameness to all" is a policy that may very well be put into practice in the East where everyone respects a trained hawk. But in this country I, for one, see nothing to complain about if a hawk jump off her block on the approach of a stranger.

FLYING TO THE LURE—USE OF THE LURE

ON seeing a lure for the first time no young falconer need be told what it is, assuming that he has acquired the most elementary knowledge of the sport, but to his hawk, that yet has to learn its use, it is a strange object whether dressed in feathers or not, and a frightening one too if first waved about in front of her. It is first brought to her notice while she is weathering. Having tied a good portion of her meal on it, keep it close in to your body, on approaching her, and simply place it on the ground at the length of her leash from the block, then retire a few paces. Blow the whistle which by now she is beginning to associate with food as, latterly, you have blown it every time you have presented her with food even though it was only a titbit. And for ever more blow it every time you show her the lure when you want her to come to it.

In a couple of days or so your hawk will jump down from the block the instant you place the lure on the ground in front of her. It is then time to begin calling her off to the lure, at increasing distances, on a creance. Three or four yards is sufficient at first. If, at any time you have been over ambitious, and she hesitate to fly the distance you have measured for her, at once pick up the lure by its cord and, with a swing, let it drop (right side uppermost) on the ground nearer to her. It only puts the brake on her progress if she is left undecided about coming to it. Every time she sees it she must come at once to it. Too much hesitation will very likely make her fly over and past the lure. That is a set-back which must be guarded against. You will of course call her up against the wind. If you call her to the lure down wind she is almost certain to fly over and past it, meaning of course to turn so as to alight on the lure against the wind, but the length of creance will not allow of this.

If your pupil take titbits nicely it is very good to slip her one or two while she feeds on the lure. If, however, she grab it ill-manneredly, almost swallowing your fist as well as the titbit, don't encourage her so to disgrace herself because she will not be a bit grateful for the attention.

If the hawk is nervous do not, in calling her off, allow the lure to drop in front of you, because she will be shy at flying directly towards you. Instead let it fall as far to the side as the lure-string will allow and do not use too short a lure-string. Always thus guard against her flying past you to be brought up on the end of the creance.

The length of the creance should be half the length of the course. Thus one end of it is tied to the hawk's swivel, where she sits on your assistant's fist, and the other is tied to a weight halfway down the course. So that when she has flown to you she is about at the end of the creance's reach. You thus have her on the minimum length of creance. Otherwise if you hold one end while she is at the other, on the man's fist, you have a creance that is twice as long as it need be. So that if anything goes wrong you will have her flying around in an alarmingly wide circle, perhaps with the hawk in danger of colliding with trees or fences. In practice the creance should be a yard or so longer than half the course to allow for any error of judgment in the placing of the lure. The weight which is placed on the ground at the halfway mark should not be so heavy as to bring the hawk down with a distressing bump if she should fly beyond the lure.

A hawk is less likely to shy at alighting on a lure if its string be held so that it lies for the most part flat on the ground, instead of being held taut, at an angle from the ground, between the lure and the hand.

In giving all this advice on what might be judged as rather trivial detail, I am anxious for only one thing, and that is the avoidance of any sort of contretemps because accidents and setbacks shake a hawk's faith in her trainer.

After your hawk has flown without the creance, and she comes one or two hundred yards against the wind without any hesitation to the swung lure and the whistle, it is time to fly her to the lure in the ordinary way. With your lure concealed in your falconer's bag you may cast her off the fist, although I think it is better to hold the fist high and let her take off in her own good time if she does not take too long about it. After she has flown round once produce the lure, swing it once or twice, let it fall at the length of its cord and whistle her down. Always see that it falls meat side uppermost, if it does not, dash in and right it before she comes near you.

As the days go by you can keep her up longer but never so long as to let her rake away.

It is sometimes advocated that the falconer keep showing the lure to keep her attention towards him. Personally I consider this a thoroughly bad practice as it always, always paves the way to future trouble. Properly used the lure is nothing more than an instrument whereby the hawk is persuaded to return to the falconer for the very practical purpose of getting something to eat. That is the way she looks at it anyway. So that for every time you show it to her and don't let her have it it loses some of its value as a signal to bring her in. Being the sensible bird that she is she will not be fooled indefinitely, so that if the young falconer persist day after day in waving it merely to keep her around, in time she will pay little attention to it and he thus greatly increases the chance of losing her. Ruefully he will have to admit to himself that instead of fooling his hawk she has made a fool of him when she turns her tail on its blandishments and flies away. Apart from all that it is apposite to point out that not only does she thus lose respect for the lure, she loses respect for the falconer too because it is a form of insincerity that she will not be slow to appraise.

Furthermore there is no excuse for this deceptive showing of the lure. It may be argued that it is a means of keeping the hawk on the wing longer, but if the extra exercise is at the expense of the lure's effectiveness there is no justification for it. Console yourself in the thought that the real exercise will come later, when you go hawking with her, for flying to the lure is not an end in itself, it merely covers the short interim while she learns its use in preparation for the more serious work ahead. While she learns its use, be it noted, so don't misuse it. Keep her on the wing until she shows the first sign of breaking her circling round you, then, while her tail is towards you as she flies away, blow a good blast on the whistle, that will turn her, then immediately produce the lure and let her have it. That is the order, first the whistle then the lure, so that she will always associate the former with the latter.

That is as far as flying to the lure will take your hawk on the road to actual hawking. She will learn nothing more from it. Continue with the lessons until you are certain that she is *au fait* with the lure's use, then get her straight on to hawking. Let no one imagine that she can be taught to wait-on through flying to the lure. No game-hawk ever created has learnt to wait-on while flying to the lure. The sole reason why a hawk waits-on is because she thereby puts herself in a position to be able to intercept fast-flying game. She has no need to fly at a thousand feet high or more to get the lure, quite the contrary. She may take to the soar and may even drift over your head at a great height while doing so, but, far from doing that for the lure she will, during her soaring, entirely ignore it and you.

Soaring is not waiting-on. The most you can do is to keep her flying round you for the lure, but that, too, is very different from waiting-on.

From the first day that a hawk is entered to quarry the lure is used simply and solely as a means for recalling her. I am aware that that statement may be challenged by a few falconers who cherish the idea of flying a hawk to the lure in the off-seasons for the sake of exercise. Personally I contend that though exercise is desirable it should not be regarded as an end in itself, which of course it is when there are no near prospects of flying her at quarry. When a hawk is fully trained the only times she should be flown, for ever after, should be at quarry. Persist in flying her to the lure in between seasons and you will probably spoil her, almost certainly you will lose her in the end. A hawk that has been flying rooks or game successfully does not consider flying to the lure good enough. If she is satisfied with stooping to the swung lure as a substitute for the real thing she is not a first-rate hawk, in which case she will probably be persuaded, by continued practise at this form of exercise, to regard it as preferable to spending her energy in counteracting the evasive tactics of the birds of the air which the swung lure cannot possibly imitate. When such a hawk is put on the wing again to fly at quarry it is disheartening in the extreme to find that she has become more lure-minded than bird-minded, and I, for one, would feel shamed to think that her natural instincts had been so perverted, because for this

129

end she was not created.

It may be fun for the falconer to stoop his hawk to the lure but I suspect that he gets more entertainment out of it than does his hawk. For her the performance is rather crooked dealing on his part, even though it always ends in her trumpery victory. It is this forever absence of ultimate defeat that tends to warp her natural instincts and cause predilection for the lure.

It is quite amusing to stoop to the lure hobbies and kestrels or any pet falcon that does not distinguish herself at quarry. I used to do it until one day, trying to get even with the smartness of an African merlin, I jerked the lure right through her wing and so smashed several flight feathers. I am not the only one to have caused such a horrible accident. I never stooped a hawk to the lure again since then. In any case I only hawk game nowadays so the practice is not applicable. You cannot stoop a game-hawk to the lure, simply because she must be encouraged to fly high instead of wasting time flying around near to the ground watching and waiting for your hand to dip into the lure bag.

In concluding this chapter it might not be out of order to refer to "cuckoo" flight because this weakness in a hawk is first demonstrated when she is first put on the wing to the lure. When a good hawk flies she carries her wings horizontally. When she races she raises them high over her back at every stroke. Cuckoo flight denotes exactly the opposite, for then she holds her wings below the level of her back and beats them lower still—in fact like a cuckoo in flight. Unhacked eyasses are particularly prone to it. I have never seen a passager or haggard guilty of this contemptible habit. It makes for slowness, in fact it is because the offending hawk intentionally flies slowly that she automatically does it. Wild hawks that have recently left the nest fly in the same way round their parents for precisely the same reason that young eyasses do it round the falconer for in both cases they expect to be provided with food, and that is why they fly "with the brakes on." As it is not a congenital weakness there is no cause for undue discouragement when you see your hawk fly like that. If she is potentially good she will fly as a decent hawk should when "all out" after quarry. The annoying habit will disappear with time as she becomes more dependent on her own powers. But if she always flies like a cuckoo it will be because she has less faith in her ability to catch her own dinner than she has in your providing it for her by means of the lure.

HAWKING

AS this is a book of personal observations I am limited to writing only on those branches of hawking that I myself have practised, indeed it would be presumptuous to include any other however well the theory be understood. I have hawked birds of the hedgerow with sparrow-hawks and have a great admiration for this very sporting, lion-hearted little hawk. I prefer her to the goshawk which has taken rabbits in plenty for me, but never a pheasant nor even a partridge. If life were not so short I would be far from finished with the sparrow-hawk. That her powers have not been fully exploited is my belief. Sometimes I almost wish that from now on circumstances would permit only of my flying this very beautiful shortwing, so that I would still have plenty of time to try her at woodcock, teal, partridge—yes, and snipe. But as I specialize in Peregrines, except when vacillating over the exciting potentialities of Gyrfalcons, I have not the opportunity to indulge all my ambitions. So I will continue to confine my observations to Peregrines which was my intention when I began writing this book. With the Peregrine falcon I have enjoyed many a day's rook hawking on Salisbury Plain before it became as badly fenced as it is to-day. I have even taken rooks and crows in enclosed country in Worcestershire where I used to farm, but not many, and then it was after the manner of magpie hawking. On this same farm I had a limited amount of partridge hawking. It was always my ambition to go in for game-hawking and the opportunity came when I went to live among the hills of South Shropshire. I rented a grouse moor and it is over this same moor that I fly my hawks to-day. The terrain is far from ideal, being too hilly, and it yearly deteriorates through the encroachment of bracken. Such conditions preclude the possibility of impressive scores at grouse, yet we get our sport, even though the season's total score of grouse and wild-duck is never more than a modest one.

It is impossible to compare rook-hawking with game-hawking, but it can be said that in both these flights one gets the full measure of the Peregrine's admirable versatility. For that reason it is desirable that a falconer experience both. I would recommend the beginner to hawk rooks before he hawks game, because the latter sport requires far more organization and a greater knowledge of the hawk herself than what the young falconer in his early days has at his command. After a few seasons' rook hawking he will have learnt much of the nature and of the management of the Peregrine in the field so will be better qualified to encounter the difficulties that attend game-hawking.

By the time the young falconer has successfully flown his hawk at rooks he will doubtless have formulated in his own mind just what is required to take pheasant, partridge, or grouse. And, really, from reading some books on the subject, game-hawking appears quite a straightforward business after all. There is no trouble about persuading his hawk to fly game because it is the natural quarry of the Peregrine. One only has to teach her to wait-on, then you can go out to the fields or the moor, mark some partridge or grouse, put the hawk up and then run in and flush the birds—and—*voilà loul!* Dogs are just a dispensable luxury. That is what I used to think, and judging by conversations I have had with beginners it appears to be a fairly common impression, and they will not be persuaded otherwise. Perhaps it is just as well that they do think like that. Let them try it, because there is no way like the haid way for gaining knowledge, then they will go ahead and build on experience.

There is no trouble in marking down game. Equally it is easy to unleash and cast oft your hawk. If she does net wait-on, and doubtless she won't at that stage of experience, she will nevertheless quite likely fly around at some little height. You rush in to where the birds were lying, and in a panic of anxiety zig-zag all over the place where they were, hoping desperately to put them up while the hawk is somewhere near. But what has happened to them, they don't get up? They never do, not until the hawk, getting tired of flying in small circles, begins flying out wider, and then, when she is some little distance away up jump the birds. They choose their own time for getting up, which never coincides with yours, and that time is always when the hawk is well away from them, for they never lose their heads and do anything foolish. The hawk sees them, more often than not, when they do get up, but by then it is too late because they have too good a start and almost always put into some distant cover where, without a dog, it is much more likely than not that they will not be found. Even if you do succeed in putting them out ultimately the hawk will have cleared off again, and she will remain with you for a shorter period than she did at first.

It is really incredible how partridge and grouse can run in the shorter stubble or heather without being seen. Very many times when I have been out with a setter, but without a spaniel, I have watched the setter's drawing on after the running birds. Its nose during those moments, apparently points them with the directness of a compass' needle. With the intention of flushing them down wind I face the dog and dash about madly over the ground between, always watching that nose for fresh indications. I *know* the grouse are there, and I *know* they are running towards me, but though the heather be only six inches high, I cannot spot any movement however close I seem to be. What always happens is that they branch out, either to the right or left of me, and fairly leg it once they have got past. The setter makes a swift advance with characteristic smooth, gliding movements and I run to head them off to get them once again between the dog and myself. If the hawk is an old campaigner and continues to wait-on obediently this exasperating business often ends with the grouse running into the sanctuary of bracken. But if she be a hawk of the year she gets sick of it all and rakes away, and then of course up jump the grouse a long way ahead with their cackling laugh of derision.

I call attention to this in support of the true statement that in game-hawking a combination of ingredients is essential to success. Take away any one of them and the whole organization breaks down and disappointment and failure is the result. I would list the essential ingredients as follows:—

(1) suitable country

(2) plenty of game

(3) a hawk that waits-on

(4) a setter and a spaniel

(5) suitable weather

in addition to the above it is sometimes recommended that men be available to serve as markers in order that the kill be more easily located. With this, however I beg to disagree because in my experience these men do more harm than good by driving away game while proceeding to take up their positions.

Let us take the essentials as listed. Suitable country. I have never had the opportunity to hawk partridges in a big way because our farm in Worcestershire was typical of what farms usually are in England, none of the fields was very large and every field was bounded by hedges. Over this sort of country it is impossible to use a high-mounting hawk because of the lack of space. Hawks used to get discouraged by the birds' forever putting in. We killed a fair number of partridge nevertheless but the sport, such as it was, rather resembled a rat-hunt as we spent too much time poking about hedges and noisily urging on the dogs to put out the birds. For the same reason it was hopeless for pheasant hawking as these birds used to run for the nearest copse the moment the hawking party entered the field. There are few areas where partridge hawking can be properly enjoyed because farm land is seldom sufficiently open. Flat, prairie-like country is the ideal such as one finds on the Wiltshire Downs.

For grouse hawking, too, the more level the country the better. Where the ground is broken by hills and valleys the flights are soon lost to sight and consequently one spends far too much time in trying to locate kills. When a grouse is pursued by a hawk it nearly always flies downhill. Thus the falconer too often finds himself at the bottom of a valley searching for a possible kill after the hawk has failed to return within ten minutes or so. Maybe the hawk has not killed and while he looks for her she may be back on the high ground again looking for him. On such a moor a hawk can be easily lost, because of this it is essential that in these conditions she be taught to "home," but that accomplishment in itself often costs a whole afternoon's hawking because the falconer, loath to call it a day, will very often waste an hour searching for her before returning home to look for her there.

Just as hedges and copses spoil partridge hawking so do belts of bracken spoil grouse hawking. Also the heather itself can be another hindrance if it is deep because grouse put in to that too, and very effectively. Either the moor must be very well burnt or better still be of that type that grows only short, scrubby heather.

So it can be understood that the areas of moorland suitable for hawking are limited. Over the flat, brackenless, short-heather type large bags can be made. Over the other kind only the very best hawks will put up any score at all. Others that would distinguish themselves in the right conditions of terrain become so discouraged in the wrong conditions that they soon cease to pursue grouse. To the falconer it is disheartening in the extreme to see potentially good grouse or partridge hawks never having a real chance because of being flown in unsuitable country. The same of course applies to pheasant hawking. This quarry can only be hawked where it is found away from woods, hedges, deep agricultural crops, deep heather and bracken. And really one has to be nearly as particular when it comes to hawking wild-duck. Generally speaking these birds do not put in to cover, other than water, yet many times I have seen them fall from the hawk's foot into cover and not be found again.

Where duck hawking is concerned it matters very much what type of water the falconer has at his disposal. Large ponds and rivers are useless because the quarry will not fly away from them, they return only to put in, and once a duck has put in to a sizeable stretch of water it is impossible to put it on the wing again. The ideal is found in small, overhung ponds. Not quite so good are winding, overgrown streams. Small ponds that lack cover afford good sport if the duck will remain on them during the day, but usually they leave them before dawn because, after their night's feeding they like to pass the daylight hours in cover, especially after they have been hawked a few times.

I have included duck hawking with game hawking because, in my opinion, this quarry affords the best sport when hawked as game as opposed to its being flown out of the hood. Let us now pass on to the next requirement on the list for successful game hawking.

Plenty of game. Where shooting is concerned a scarcity of birds is bad enough, but at least the shooting man and his friends can still have an enjoyable afternoon's walking even if they bag only a brace between them, or none at all. In the much more exacting sport of hawking, however, positive harm is done the hawk if she wait-on unrewarded. Waiting-on is not, as some people imagine, just an idle soaring over the falconer's head, for the times and the places where a hawk can spread her wings and "sit on the breeze" and follow the falconer for a mile, if need be, are extremely limited. Waiting-on for her is nearly always really hard work. She must use her wings all the time to keep up. She must keep turning so that she will not drift from the falconer and his dogs, and that tires her. Wild hawks suffer no such restriction. If she has one or two successful seasons behind her at game one or two blank afternoons of course will not spoil her, but if there be too much repetition of birdless days she will give up waiting-on, for waiting-on is an act of faith in the falconer's ability to flush birds for her.

On the other side of the picture we have a young eyass, or a recently-caught passager or haggard, that has not long been taught to wait-on. The setter points, the hawk is put up, but the point is a false one and there are no birds so the hawk is tamely brought down to the lure. Repetition of this sort of thing very soon spoils her. A false point is not so serious where game abounds because the falconer and dogs, without taking the hawk down, only have to hurry on to be reasonably certain of putting something up before they have gone far.

Where game is scarce hawking is a heart-breaking business. The shooting man can be quite happy enjoying the walk over stubble or heather, but the falconer has his hawk to think about and it does not please him to see her patiently breasting the breeze, hooded, on his fist, while he anxiously watches the ranging setter, hoping and praying for a point. And as the weary miles are covered without reward he debates, miserably, whether to feed her up or whether to put her on the wing to the lure merely for the sake of exercise. In either case a degree of harm is done.

How different is the picture where birds are abundant! As the hawk goes on from kill to kill, day after day, the partnership between her and her friends, the falconer and his dogs, draws always closer. As her confidence in her own powers grows she becomes more and more the master performer while the falconer becomes increasingly free to enjoy the sport as a spectator. Surely the ancient adage "Nothing succeeds like success" must have referred originally to game-hawking! And as the season draws on what a holiday feeling it gives one to be able to put the hawk up to wait-on at the commencement of the walk over the moor in the certain knowledge that you won't have to go far before birds are flushed!

Assuming that the falconer has plenty of game on his ground he must make sure that he has a hawk good enough for this flight. It is a poor Peregrine that cannot catch a partridge early in the season, in suitable country, in a straight chase. Indeed she ought to be able to catch them when they get up, wild and wide, in October. Grouse, however, are faster and much harder to stop. Only once in my life have I had a falcon good enough to catch them, on the flat, in October. It made me proud of her to know that she could do this, but all my unbounded admiration, for this particular hawk, was for her glorious stoop from a very high waiting-on pitch. Had I merely flown her at the bolt it would have been sheer prostitution of her wonderful ability. No real falconer would contemplate flying a Peregrine at game in so unworthy a fashion, that is why, for game-hawking, a hawk that will wait-on is a *sine qua non*.

Game-hawking is the highest expression of the falconer's art. Waiting-on is the most impressive part of it. Therein is the real test of his ability to train a hawk. Therein is the real measure of his hawk's faith in him as an ally of the chase. It is an exhibition in itself. In no other way does a hawk demonstrate so well the fact that it is trained. The Peregrine is justly famed for her dramatic stoop, in no other way can she put it to such good effect as when she is taught to wait-on.

There is only one way to teach a hawk to wait-on and that is by your repetitive flushing of birds under her. She will show signs of waiting-on as soon as she learns by experience that she can expect you to do this. When she can *rely* upon your doing so it will have become a confirmed habit.

This is stating what should be the obvious, but I make no apology for putting it down because, rather surprisingly, there does seem to linger some confusion of thought on the subject. Looking back over my early days I must admit that I once cherished the hope of persuading hawks to wait-on where there was very little game. I could put up partridges, with the hawk in the air, but only every other day or nearly so, and, surely, I thought, by filling in the gaps with the lure that ought to do the trick. But it did not, nor will it ever in such conditions.

Use of the lure certainly does pave the way to waiting-on in so far as it teaches the hawk to fly round the falconer, but the first day birds are flushed under the hawk must be followed by more birds being flushed under her every succeeding day, and there must be no interspersing of days when she is flown only to the lure. With this treatment the hawk, if a good one, will, in time, wait-on, any modification of it will attract disappointment.

When the first few weeks of lessons in waiting-on tally with the opening of the game season she has the indispensable advantage of being able to hawk young and moulting old birds that will lie to the setter's point. Thus you first find your birds pin them down with the dogs nose and then, not before, put up the hawk. In these early days she cannot be expected to mount, it is enough that she is in the air, and once she is in the air it must be your object to flush the birds, with the spaniel, the first time she flies over the dog. It requires very nice timing and needless to add it is of paramount importance that the birds be flushed down wind. If they are grouse and they fly up wind she will be a very exceptional hawk if she catches one, and grouse always will fly up wind if they get half a chance, as they know so very well that in that direction lies their best chance of escape.

The method of countering grouse's determination to fly up wind calls for a special paragraph, even so I doubt whether I will be able to emphasize sufficiently its importance. Somehow, in the excitement of having a hawk in the air and grouse down below in the heather, one gets careless, when that happens the birds *always* fly up wind and everything is spoilt. So I earnestly beg the beginner's closest attention to the description of the disciplinary drill that must be carried out to the last letter.

On a point being made the hawk is cast off. For a moment the field must remain quite still until she has flown somewhere near the crouching birds. This is to hold them down. Then the falconer, with his friend, must run round the dog's nose in a wide circuit so that there will be no possible chance of flushing the birds prematurely The man in charge of the dogs may want to stop behind with the setter but on no account may he be allowed to do so, he must run round too, closely followed by the spaniel which he must keep well in to heel. Thus the field ends the race (for no time must be lost when a hawk, new to the business, is up) fifty yards or so up wind of the dog's nose. They spread out in a line to form a screen, the falconer in the centre, opposite the dog, flanked by the others at fifteen or twenty yard intervals. The line of men must be strictly at right angles to the direction of the wind or in other words it must be blowing straight into their backs. Thus a screen is formed through which it is hoped the birds, when flushed, will not pass, being compelled to fly down wind. The falconer breathlessly watches his hawk, and when she is flying in towards the field he gives the signal for the spaniel to be sent in. *Only* the spaniel dashes in, the field remain perfectly still. On the spaniel's flushing the birds every man shouts and waves his arms as an extra inducement to the grouse to fly down wind. Thus the hawk is presented with the maximum opportunity of making a kill.

It is all very simple really, but actually what too often happens is that one of the field, unable to bear the suspense of the spaniel's nosing about after the birds, and fearful that the hawk fly away again, dashes in too. Thus a gap in the screen of men is made through which the birds invariably fly—up wind. He nearly always runs right through the birds so that they rise behind him.

I mention this because we are concerned with teaching a hawk to wait-on and this is one of the surest ways of making her disgusted with the whole performance if not carried out properly. The same applies to partridge and pheasant. An up-wind stoop, even though it hit the target, lacks the speed, drive and punch of a down-wind one. Almost certainly a bird will pick itself up from an up-wind stoop and, in its extremity, heedless of the shouting and gesticulating field who are powerless to prevent it, will fly with certainty into the wind. The hawk will chase it, accompanied by the loud groans of frustration from the watching men who know very well that she will be outflown, for a grouse bores into the wind at a speed that enables it to out-distance its pursuer. Whereas on the other hand a downwind stoop is clean and hard and killing and it is effective over a long distance when birds get up wild and wide. In it one can see the Peregrine at her very best.

After the first few weeks birds will have become too wild to lie to the setter's point. By that time the hawk should have advanced sufficiently in her lessons, and in her understanding of the part she performs in the sport, for the falconer to be able to trust her to wait-on while the setter ranges. Her presence on the wing will prevent the birds from getting up until the right moment arrives for flushing them. During these days the hawk will have acquired some height in her waiting-on and the falconer will watch her with dawning pride while she beats up and down, for he will know that she, for her part, is keeping an eye on the dog, for by now she is beginning to understand that quadruped's part in the sport. Later on she will know the full meaning of a point. But these are anxious days too, because as yet the falconer dare not keep her up more than a few minutes. Therefore the field will advance at the double so as to keep up with the fast, wide-ranging dog and be ready to put birds up with a minimum of delay after a point is made. It is imperative that a covey be located soon otherwise the hawk will spread her wings and go her own way which will not be where the falconer wants her to be. It is a sight that fills him with dismay, for he well knows that she only has to do this a few times for all his patient work to be undone, therefore, at the first dim hint of wavering she *must* be served. It is well to have noted previously by ear or eye, that the area to be flown over really does contain birds before the hawk is put up.

With the wearing on of the season the falconer's anxiety recedes as his hawk becomes confirmed in the habit of waiting-on. By that time her score in the game-book will be steadily increasing if she is as good as we want her to be. She will know by then that game-birds are well within her powers, and in this assurance she will not be unduly discouraged when, either through the vagaries of the weather or any other reason, the falconer fail to find birds for her. Indeed it is even possible that, at that late stage, such an occasional blank day may serve to broaden her outlook on the sport. Her new conception of it may lead her increasingly to enjoy flying for flying's sake so that she goes up to greater heights where the exhilaration of a greater sense of freedom will compensate for the lack of that profitable activity down below her that she has been led to expect.

I have seen evidence of this, but it happens only with hawks of outstanding brilliance and they are in a very small minority. Such I have seen, on rare occasions, that were so obsessed with their high flying, even where a cold, strong wind has been blowing, that it seemingly required almost an effort for them to turn their attention earthwards to a covey of grouse flushed in a last despairing minute.

But it would be the greatest mistake to assume that hawks of such excellence would continue to wait-on daily simply for the sake of that exercise. They may be carried away momentarily through sheer enjoyment of it, but in the main it will continue to be for them a profitable form of hunting in association with man and dog. Therefore while your hawk flies high, a mere speck in the heavens, let us hope, she is waiting on you. It is in every sense the highest compliment she can pay you, therefore you are under the greatest obligation to fulfil your part of the contract.

Passing on to the fourth requirement for game-hawking we come to the subject of dogs. There is no need to stress their importance because it would be impossible to hawk without them. It is a necessity, not a luxury, to have both setter and spaniel. Let anyone try to teach a hawk to wait-on with only one or the other and he will then understand what I mean. Maybe there is a unique strain of setter, or pointer, that will do a spaniel's work as well as its own, but, if there is, no dog of this kind has ever come my way. If the setter be encouraged to run in and put birds up this will spoil it for holding its point, for it is absolutely essential that it remain resolutely on point while the field manœuvres to take up their positions for flushing the birds down-wind. Putting the birds up is of course left to the spaniel, and it will do this with a speed, sureness and directness that no human being could possibly emulate.

If the falconer is to succeed in game-hawking he has to

be a perfectionist, therefore only the best dogs can be used. Everything else being equal good dogs will make good hawks, but unreliable dogs will spoil any hawk's chances. The sport is so exacting that it allows but very little margin of error on the dogs' part. It has been said that a setter, or a spaniel, works more intelligently with hawks than with guns. I am not a shooting man so cannot confirm this, but I have been very impressed by the helpful behaviour of Mr. William Humphrey's famous field trial champion setters, and I would like to add in gratitude that I am always impressed by Mr. Humphrey's kindness, not only for allowing me to use his dogs, but also for his running them himself under my hawks. Dogs and hawks appear as a harmonious natural partnership. It is amusing to watch a setter on point slyly turning its head to ascertain the position of the hawk above. And how gratifying it is to see the spaniel drop to the raised hand when the hawk goes wide! Such restraint when its nose is about to push up the birds is a severe test on its obedience but I believe it does this with complete understanding.

A false point or two is of no consequence when shooting is the sport, but a setter that so errs in hawking can spoil a young hawk. It must not false-point. It must move fast, must range far and wide so as to find birds in the shortest possible time.

The first requirement for the spaniel is obedience. It must keep well in to heel, must dash forward when commanded and must keep one eye on the falconer all the time for signals.

Under normal conditions dogs are always worked against the wind. The setter naturally likes it this way so it can use its nose to the best effect. Later on in the season, however, when the weather deteriorates birds get so wild that coveys of them keep rising well ahead of the ranging setter. To cope with the wildness of game the hawk by now has to be put on the wing before the setter's ranging begins, but it is discouraging to her to have birds springing up nearly a quarter of a mile in front and pushing on up against the wind. To deal with this situation I use the dogs in an unorthodox way that would scandalize a true dog-man. I work them down-wind. For the first few days of this change of tactics the setter is apt to make repeated attempts to get round into the wind, but before very long it yields to the new law, and romps about down-wind quite happily, sometimes running into a point out of which the spaniel, in the absence of any restraint, is quick to produce a display of rising birds that appear to get torn out of the ground by the wind's pressure, to streak away down the wind, provided that the advancing field keep a well-spaced line.

It is at this time, I think, that hawking is at its very finest. There is less for the field to worry about, no points of dog to run round, just a steady advance of the line of men who are now free to enjoy the sport in the luxurious rôle of spectators in the absence of any special manœuvering on their part.

If the falconer has successfully brought his hawk along the

path of training to this new development, that the end-of-season's roughness of weather and wildness of game call for, he can consider that he has now brought her to the climax that will end all doubt as to her degree of quality as a game hawk. Few hawks are brave enough to ride a half-gale, the best glory in it and in the lethal slashing stoops that it lends them to cut the birds down so cleanly in the fleetingest puff of feathers—*thump* to the ground. If his hawk prove herself to be one of those few he must thank her and Providence as well as his own skill in training her up to that pitch of excellence, for he has a treasure beyond price.

In her second season a good game-hawk will be better than ever, waiting-on higher, more steadily and for longer periods. It is as if she had mentally digested the experiences of her first season during the months of moulting inactivity. Anyway in her second she takes the field as an expert and at once shows her trainer that she has forgotten nothing. In her he has a hawk perfectly adapted to a specialized form of hunting. From then on his principal preoccupation will be to serve her with game. She will supply most of the resourcefulness necessary to deal with it, and so leave him free to transfer his anxiety to another young hawk of the year.

As the years go by the falconer will get into the way of regarding young hawks, at the commencement of each season, as average, above-average, and below-average. As the weeks pass they will develop one way or the other so that he will class them either as good hawks or bad hawks. Some of the good ones, profiting by their success, will become very good. Whereas the bad ones will rely upon the falconer and his lure more and more, with diminishing faith in their own ability to catch anything that flies.

And now the last on the list of essential ingredients for game or, for that matter, any other kind of hawking, suitable weather. As just stated the boisterous weather of late autumn can be tolerated and enjoyed when hawks fly high and are in every way made to the sport, so long as it is not too boisterous, for most Peregrines object to waiting-on when half a gale is blowing. Early in the season, however, when young hawks have to be taught, reasonably fine weather with light or moderate breezes is a necessity. Without this condition a hawk will hardly be persuaded to learn to wait-on.

*   *   *

And now for some general remarks on hawking. When hawks are being entered to their quarry the falconer should resist the entreaties of numerous friends who may want to accompany him. It is a time for quietness and orderliness and that is hardly to be found where more than two or three are gathered together. During her previous weeks of training a hawk will not have been accustomed to a crowd of people, so that it would be courting disaster for her to be confronted by them at a time when she can be more easily marred than made.

At all times the attentions of people have to be guarded against. One would think that when a hawk is about to be unhooded, as a preliminary to casting her off, that spectators would have the good sense to stand back so that she will not leave the fist in a bate, but instead of showing such consideration they usually crowd forward. And when the hawk is in the air the falconer must not allow people to stand round him or walk with him. He must remember that he is the falconer and as such must stand out alone where he is unmistakeable to his hawk above instead of being mixed up with other people.

I refer more particularly to a hawk's early days of flying. Later on she will have become gradually accustomed to a sizeable field so that the falconer can then afford to relax somewhat in such matters. Even so he will be wise to brief new spectators to the sport before starting out. Had I always had the sense to have taken this precaution more than one disaster would have been averted. It is unpleasant to have to shout at a spectator who is fool enough to rush up to a hawk on her kill and frighten her off. It is upsetting, to say the least, when one is busy in taking up a hawk, to have her suddenly fly off in a fright because someone had crept up behind you with a camera. One would have thought that in producing the lure to call a hawk down anyone with a modicum of consideration would give ground to the falconer in case she is shy about coming to the lure with a stranger or two standing close by, but too often it has been my unhappy experience either to have to make what should have been an unnecessary request to people to withdraw, or else to run away often with them in close pursuit. So it can be seen that a little quiet talk to strangers to the sport before starting out is a wise precaution. To the list of sins that casual spectators are addicted to I would add loud talking. Wild birds hate the sound of the human voice and it does not help matters to have them taking wing all over the place prematurely because people talk too much. The falconer can be relied upon to keep his eye on the setter so there is no need for a chorus of voices to announce a point. Neither is it necessary for raised arms to indicate where the point is, for this sudden movement often puts birds on the wing when they are required to stay on the ground. A hawking party is not a hurrah party except just at that exciting moment when game rise with a hawk over them, only then and not before is the field permitted to shout, just a sharp, short shout, not a long drawn-out one or it will be impossible to hear the hiss of the hawk's stoop which is one of the most thrilling things in the whole sport of hawking. The shout really is necessary to draw a hawk's attention to a rising covey because, so often, birds choose just that moment to rise when the hawk has her head pointed in the opposite direction. Hawks very soon learn what a shout means and it is heartening to see their sudden swing round in response to it.

Never allow any members of the field to lag behind because they are very likely to attract the hawk to wait-on over them instead of over the right place.

On the falconer's own ground no one must get in front of him, for it is his responsibility to judge how near the field may draw up to a point, when working up-wind, without flushing the birds prematurely. The field must follow quietly ten yards or so behind him and not string out all over the place.

Where game is abundant it can be quite profitable to cruise around in a car in order to spot a covey. When birds have been marked down it is a mistake to dismount anywhere near them unless it happens to be early in the season. But when they have become strong on the wing they will not suffer the erupting of a carload of people and dogs within a hundred yards or more without taking wing prematurely. Even when the dismounting is done at a discreet distance birds have an annoying habit of jumping into flight the same second as the hawk leaves the fist, for they are artful enough to know that they can escape her more easily then instead of waiting for her to get above them. In these circumstances the best plan is to take advantage of any rise in the ground that there may be. Once the car is behind it the party may dismount, but please caution your friends not to slam the car door as the bang would probably put the birds up. By the time the party has advanced over the rise the hawk, in all probability, will be by then sufficiently high in the air to keep the birds down.

If the falconer is lucky enough to have ground on which there is no cover in which birds can put in, so that a hawk is reasonably certain to kill when game is flushed, he can make more than one kill with the same hawk in an afternoon, or morning, without doing her any harm. But if the ground be otherwise he must be very careful about this. At all times he will be loath to take his hawk down to the lure after a spell of waiting-on, and the more times he flies her the greater the likelihood that he will be compelled to bring her flying to such a tame conclusion, to her great disgust. So that in indifferent country he will be wise to feed her up after she has killed, particularly if the kill follow on one or two disappointments.

Over ground that is not ideal for hawking but where game is abundant I recommend keeping a hawk on the wing until she has killed. This procedure is infinitely preferable to taking her down to the lure with the intention of trying again later. During the time she is up birds will be getting up under her, and, though they put in, their frequent rising will be enough to hold her attention to the field and the dogs. When she finally does kill the experience will have taught her that prolonged waiting-on is a profitable exercise. And when she has killed, after putting in several coveys, it would be unwise to risk flying her again that day for fear that she may tire before she kill a second time. It is disheartening to see covey after covey putting in at a distance that makes any attempt impracticable to run up and put them out again, but how grateful one feels, and what fresh hope arises, on seeing the same hawk patiently ringing up again in preparation for the next attempt! Many an afternoon I have had like this when the initial pleasurable anticipation has been followed by disappointment after disappointment, when sustained excitement has been sharpened by agonizing anxiety lest a goodly spell of waiting-on go unrewarded. And when the hawk finally kills no power on earth would persuade me to put her up again for fear I might be robbed of that exquisite moment, that lies in store, when I put her on the perch for the night in quiet contemplation of her prolonged and high flying and of the splendid and just reward that came at the end of it.

I have written at some length on coping with conditions that arise from hawking over terrain that is not ideal because most of us, I fear, have little opportunity of doing otherwise. Plenty has been written in other books on how to hawk over perfect hawking country, but their authors write for a privileged few. I am offering guidance, for what it is worth, to the comparative many. Success is comparatively easy on flat, open country where there is no cover, such as the giants in the hawking world enjoyed in the latter half of the last century and the early decades of this. But in the conditions that are available to most modern falconers it can be truly said that it is better to be content with the modicum of success that keeps their hawks sharpened by encouragement than to risk all for a big score of kills and have that vain hope sunk in failure.

Anyway, looking at it in the best possible light, the problems that confront those of us who hawk in second-rate country are of absorbing interest. They certainly do make us think, even if too much in the realm of theory.

Here is something that I have never tried but hope to someday. I put it down in case somebody else would like to try it. Very likely someone else has already thought of it. It is in relation to this vexed question of game putting in. The idea is to bring up a hawk and a spaniel, or preferably a dog with a bit more leg on it, in such close friendship that the hawk, at all times and in all circumstances, is completely fearless of the dog. And the dog so respects the hawk that it could be trusted never, under any circumstances, to do her any harm. This happy partnership would act in this way. On game being flushed the dog would race in the direction the birds had taken so that it would quickly be on the spot to put them out wherever they put in and so keep serving the hawk until she kills. The falconer would eventually find his hawk on its quarry with the dog lying near her. A nice elaboration of course would be for the dog to return to the falconer and lead him to the kill!

Something else that I have tried, with some success, concerns hawking with only a setter when an obedient spaniel has not been available. When the setter points fire a gun to put up the birds. The ruse has the advantage that you can flush birds exactly at the time you choose when the hawk is nicely placed. The hawk does not mind the report of the gun and quickly gets used to it. One does not like mixing shooting with hawking on ethical grounds, but if you can overcome this distaste, which I for one cannot, there is another use for the gun. If you have a hawk which, by sheer bad luck, has not killed day after day, and is so discouraged that she shows all the signs of giving up, as a last resort put a gun under your arm when you next fly her and shoot a bird under her. A day or two of this treatment might be the means of saving her. Similarly a few shot rooks might turn a hesitant hawk into a rook hawk.

But leaving behind us such dark practices and returning, with relief, to the pure art of Falconry, there seems to be a prevalent belief that tiercels are better than falcons for partridge-hawking. A good tiercel is a beautifully neat flier and there is something about his appearance that suggests the flight at partridge. Without doubt the best of them are fully equal to good falcons at this flight, but they are definitely not better. Because a tiercel often has a more alert appearance and is quicker in its movements young falconers commonly get the impression that it is also faster on the wing than a falcon. The reverse, however, is the case. The falcon is a faster bird than the tiercel. Having flown them together so often, and having had so many opportunities of seeing their racing against each other after the same quarry I have now no doubt that the falcon is the faster of the two. Nevertheless a good, high-flying tiercel is just about perfect for partridge, teal and woodcock. He is too small for pheasant and mallard, and though big enough to tackle grouse his sister is infinitely to be preferred for this flight.

I have taken only a few grouse with tiercels. Having tried both eyasses and haggards I find that they have not the weight and the drive behind their stoop to deliver a knock-out blow. They bound to young grouse all right, but when they cut fully-grown birds down these always got up again and always succeeded in saving themselves in the sanctuary of cover. I do not know but suspect that where, in rare instances, they have put up good scores at grouse it was on moors that were free of bracken and deep heather so that, having knocked the quarry down, they were able to catch them finally at the end of the straight chase that followed.

It is my experience that even falcons have to be of good average size and weight to deliver a death blow. Last season I had the pleasure of watching Mr. Geoffrey Pollard's intermewed eyass falcon flying her second season at grouse on my moor. She waited-on very high, but being slightly under average size, most of the forty-odd birds that she cut down got up again to save themselves in bracken. It is possible that she came down a little too far behind so that some of the impetus from her stoop was spent at the moment of hitting her grouse. It is also possible that she tailed it instead of catching it a blow where neck joins body. However this may be there is little doubt that had she been a few ounces heavier few, if any, of those grouse would have got up again. For partridge she would have been absolutely ideal. Grouse are exceedingly tough birds and are only very temporarily inconvenienced by a hawk's stoop that does not put them right out.

I like a falcon that is large, powerful and heavy. If I dare presume to criticize the Peregrine I should say that, wonderful and admirable bird though she is, I would like her to be a little larger so that heavier weight would give her greater speed and a harder stoop. As she is, a good falcon has grouse nicely within her powers, but she is only just equal to mallard, not quite powerful enough for blackgame and definitely too small for anything between herring gulls and wild geese unless she be one of those rare exceptions one occasionally hears about. If only she weighed three pounds instead of from two pounds two ounces to two pounds eight ounces I think she would be ideal. May I go further than that and say that if only the great Gyrfalcons could be trained with the same ease and as effectively as Peregrines *those* would be *the* hawks.

I have seen many good grouse falcons jib at the flight at mallard. I have seen eyasses, with the raw courage of youth, hotly pursue the first ducks they encounter. And I have later seen the same hawks either blink or, more often, refuse this quarry altogether, having previously been severely punished on the ground by the ducks' beating wings that are very rough indeed in the nervous reaction following on death.

But falcons that are large and powerful enough to fly mallard with success provide what is probably the finest sport to be obtained in Britain. I cannot imagine a worthier quarry. It is powerful, tireless and very fast. By far the best way is to fly it as for game—from a waiting-on pitch. Should it elude the stoop it invariably takes the air, not by a laborious ringing up but by swift and direct ascent. It taxes the hawk's powers to the utmost so that it is with acute anxiety and excitement that the field watches the two of them, the hunter and the hunted, as they sweep the sky at vast heights. I have on occasions seen the duck struck high in the air and come tumbling down to earth, turning over and over as it fell. She is an exceptionally good hawk that is not outflown by them.

HOMING

IN writing a book on hawking it is usual to give advice on how to recover lost hawks and plenty has been written on the subject. But equally important is the prevention of their loss. One of the most useful aids in giving effect to this is in teaching hawks to return to a certain place when they get away from the falconer. In most cases the hawk, if properly cared for, has no more wish to lose the falconer than he has to lose her. I repeat "in most cases" for there does come a time, notably in the autumn and in February and March, when hawks feel the migratory instinct. Trained Peregrines do not necessarily react to this instinct, but it is there and the falconer must take it into account when he goes hawking. When, at other times, he has no cause for uneasiness when his hawk gets out of sight he must, during migration periods, give himself no rest while distance and time separates her from him. His hawk may be very much attached to him and probably his fears of losing her are groundless, but the real danger comes if she should happen to associate with another hawk, a wild one, while she is away. I have had hawks which have flown away with wild ones. Once when I was hawking in Ireland my falcon flew off with a wild tiercel. It was in Frebruary. After spending three days away with him she returned to me. It would have been less surprising if she had not. I could recount many instances of my trained hawks leaving me in the migration season. Often they have returned after a short or long absence, but seldom have they done so on those occasions when it was confirmed that they were in company with other hawks.

Hawks in the wild form an attachment for their own home rocks where they breed. According to my observations and those of other people our resident Peregrines are tied to their nesting localities for regular and irregular periods throughout the year. From February until June they are constantly in the neighbourhood of the eyrie. After that their visits to it are irregular, but from time to time they keep turning up in its vicinity.

Falconers can make use of the Peregrine's partiality for a certain place in regard to the prevention of losing trained hawks. Firstly by always flying them over the same ground and, secondly, by making a certain place on that ground attractive to them. In the latter case it is a great help if the falconer's home is where he hawks. If his house have buildings and trees, or better still rocks, near it he can ask for nothing better, because in such a place a hawk at liberty can find comfortable foothold and shelter from wind. But supposing his home is some distance away from his hawking ground then I would advise him to select a suitable spot on that ground which he can regard as his headquarters. A sheltered cliff, a ruined house, or even a copse, if it have wide-spreading trees

164

in it, will serve his purpose providing no alien human activity goes on near such places. Whichever spot he selects there he will begin to fly his hawks from their earliest days, to the lure. He will note their choice of perching places and allow them to become familiar with them. As the days pass he will fly them progressively farther away, and he will note with satisfaction that if he delay showing the lure his hawks will tend to return "home" to rest on a favourite perching place. It is a good thing to encourage this and for the falconer not to give a hawk the lure until he himself has returned home. A hawk will patiently wait for the hire when she sees him on foot, in the distance, homeward bound.

When the falconer begins to fly his hawk at rooks or game he will be wise to do so as near "home" as possible. Sooner or later he will leave her out, though not, of course, by design. She may be away an hour, maybe for the remainder of the day and the night that follows, but almost certainly she will return if she had previously received her full course of homing lessons. How rewarding to the falconer is that first return after a hawk's temporary loss! How triumphantly will he shout "She's horned!" knowing that what she has achieved once she can reasonably be expected to repeat on future occasions. I am fortunate enough to live in a cottage right in the middle of my hawking moor. Within fifty yards of it is a tree with a bare branch at the top. It is not the only tree and there are the roofs of outbuildings and of the cottage itself which, however, only rarely tempt a hawk to take perch. The dead branch offers the highest perch of the lot and there the hawks repair. A window in the cottage looks out to this tree. When a hawk is "out" and when I am in the cottage my gaze is fastened to this window. We talk, we have our meals, and all the time I am looking through the window. The dead branch looks more bare than ever until that joyous moment when it is suddenly crossed by the form of a hawk. If the hawk is an old "homer" there is no need for haste, but if she is new and her absence has caused uneasiness, the tea-cups fly and the chair is thrown to the ground in what I trust my companions, who read this, regard as pardonable excitement, though for all I care they can think me just mad. I kill a pigeon and take her down to a warm feed. Always thus reward a homed hawk. Give her rabbit on such occasions and she will become less keen about returning.

This homing business has one snag. Sometimes a hawk will get too fond of it. Thus if any contretemps happen out hawking, while the hawk is on the wing, she will fly home, and if she be the only hawk being flown there is nothing further that the field can in but turn about and follow her example. I have often had hawks fly home because they considered the weather not good enough for hawking. Often after a fairly long spell of waiting-on, when either no game has been sprung or birds have too frequently put in, groans have gone up from the field as the hawk has broken the rhythm of her high flying to pursue a direct line towards home. I add my own invective which later I withdraw when she flies out from home to meet me on my return. After all, one can't have it every way.

Even a passager can be taught to home, as I have proved. I once had one, a falcon, which became so attached to my moorland cottage that I was able to leave her at liberty for the greater part of the day, for nearly the whole of one season, at the end of which I gave her away because, as might be supposed, she was not much good.

When one has eyasses to deal with it is of course a very great help, in regard to homing, if they have been hacked on the spot.

Having previously warned my readers against the abuse of the lure, I am doing no right-about turn when I now tell them that when a hawk is "at home" she may be flown to it on those days when the weather is not good enough for hawking. When it is too windy for waiting-on she can be turned loose for a few minutes and then, at a blast of the whistle, brought down to the lure. The same proceeding, if carried out away from home, would be harmful because out over her hunting area she would naturally expect to fly quarry. At home, however, she has been educated to look to the lure for her food. So long as the falconer is very careful to make this distinction the homing scheme thus offers another very great advantage, for to be able to give a hawk a "breather" during patches of bad weather when hawking is impracticable is to maintain her standard of fitness. But please note this must be regarded as a concession. Hawks would be spoilt, and probably lost in the end if it became a regular practice over the months in between the hawking seasons.

THE MOULT

IT is sometimes recommended that hawks be turned loose in a loft or shed to moult. It is claimed that they thereby get a certain amount of exercise. They do, of a kind, but not the kind that is going to benefit them much, for when, ultimately, they are put on the wing again they will be found to be every bit as much short of breath as hawks that have been moulted at the block. It would have to be a huge shed that would allow any real flying.

I cannot see that a moulting shed has any advantage. It sometimes gets unhealthily hot and stuffy and is rarely free from bacteria-holding dust which cannot be good for hawks' lungs. It is not even particularly convenient for the falconer because he has daily to remove and wash away mutes if the place is not to become unhealthily dirty. It is really less trouble to take a hawk out of the mews in the morning, tie her to the block and put her on her perch again for the night. Does a hawk moult more thoroughly or faster in a shed? Not according to my experience, or if she does the very slight gain is off-set by her temporary wildness when she is brought once again into the outside world after being shut away.

Personally I know of no better way of moulting a hawk than at the block during the day-time and in an open mews

169

at night. By this method she breathes fresh air all the time and gets sufficient handling by the falconer to keep her tame. Thus if she is a first-season hawk she will be on even more familiar terms with the falconer at the end of the moult than she was at its beginning. Every time the falconer takes her on his fist it is to her advantage. She enjoys being taken out in the morning, she appreciates his moving her later into the shade, and she likes to be taken to the bath. All these gratifying little attentions she misses when relegated to the loft. And in the fulness of time she will be flying better than ever. That seems illogical after so much inactivity, but it is a fact that we must accept gratefully as no doubt she does.

One should hood a moulting hawk once daily to keep her used to it, either in the morning when taking her out, or in the evening when bringing her in. Personally I think the latter is the better time because if she is hooded always with a roof over her head she might jib at the hood outside after so long an interval when the flying season starts again.

In my opinion it is best to let a moulting hawk feed herself. It is good for her to take a long time over her meal and beneficial for her to have it on the ground so that she swallows particles of soil, little stones and bits of herbage that adhere to the meat. It is an opportunity for her to follow closely the wild hawk's feeding conditions. Domestic pigeons and chickens, woodpigeons, grey squirrels and an occasional rabbit shot with a rifle are the sort of food she needs. Let her have all that she can eat. She needs variety. Give her birds with all their feathers on and squirrels and portions of rabbit with the skin on. The more work she has to do in preparing her food before eating it the longer it will keep her amused and the more it will keep her beak from overgrowing. Prolonged feeding is an aid to good digestion and is excellent for her muscles. It is bad to give just a lump of meat that can be quickly and too easily eaten. To keep her in the best possible health her appetitie needs to be kept at that level where she is prepared to wrestle with tough skin, fur, feather, and bone to get her daily meal.

Always make the liver of every carcase available to moulting hawks. They crave it, probably because they have special need of the vitamin B and iron that it contains. In such large livers as chickens' and rabbits' it is well first to cut out the bitter gall bladder. Another penchant is the milky udder of a doe rabbit. This is best cut into strips with the fur on for casting. These are greedily swallowed and surely the valuable properties of the milk must be very beneficial. If the udder be given whole to be torn up much of the milk gets lost and the hawk gets herself into rather a mess. It would probably be dangerous to give udder that is not absolutely fresh.

If falcons and goshawks be fed in accordance with the foregoing they will grow perfect feather and will moult regularly, beginning in April and finishing in September. If they be fed on butchers' meat and rabbit they will grow brittle, lustreless feather and will moult irregularly, so that there will scarcely be a month in the year when they are not growing feathers.

Immediately before the feed shift the block to clean ground so that the food will not come into contact with mutes. Short turf is the best ground on which to weather a moulting hawk because the summer's sun will do much to neutralize any infection in the mutes that are exposed to its rays. Another advantage of short turf is that it is clear of long strands of grass which if freely swallowed with the meat can be dangerous. See that she has not access to pine needles when feeding and especially to yew which has a reputation for being poisonous. When throwing food to a moulting hawk blow the whistle so that she will continue to associate it with food.

Never leave a hawk to pant in hot sunshine.

Some hawks will voluntarily swallow rangle occasionally so provide little heaps of river gravel, small size, from time to time.

I have never tried any of the nostrums sometimes recommended for bringing a hawk quickly into flying condition again at the end of the moult. They seem so drastic. Not being a believer in short cuts in this connection I prefer to let time, dieting and exercise effect the desired result instead of pushing things down a hawk's throat. One has to be very careful about reducing the intake of food because just at this time a hawk's health can easily be seriously upset. I have known a few of them to start screaming when their food has been noticeably reduced, hawks that have never screamed before. It is a sure sign of some mistake in dieting. At first it is better to alter the quality of the food rather than the quantity, and this is where rabbit comes in so usefully. It is strange that moulting hawks, so full of fat, should become apparently ravenously hungry after a few days of rationing, yet they do, and this condition must be heeded or possibly irreparable harm will be the result.

If the intention be to kill a partridge on September the first it would not be too early to start exercising a hawk in the first week in August even though her moult will not be completed by then. She should be flown at the place to which she has been taught to home and allowed to perch when she wants to and then brought down to the lure. She will be very short of wind for some time so that the amount of flying she does must be carefully regulated from the beginning and do not let her pant too much in hot weather. The whole process of getting her back into condition should be done gradually, in her own good time. It is a gentle leading on.

HEALTH

BEFORE warning a beginner in Falconry of the diseases that may afflict his hawk I would prefer to caution him on his own attitude to the subject. Peregrines are hardy birds. In most cases if your hawks or mine sicken to the extent that their field performance is impaired it is our own fault. Prevention is relatively easy, whereas a cure that leaves a bird as good as it was before is rarely attained. A man who has but little knowledge of hawk diseases because, owing to proper conditions, disease does not often come his way, is usually a better falconer than he who claims an extensive knowledge of the treatment of the ills that seemingly bedevil the maintenance of his hawks.

It is understandable of course that in our anxiety for the hawks under our care we may become "disease conscious." That is a danger in itself if it leads to our pushing pills down the throats of hawks that look well, fly well, and eat well. In doing that we are apt to ignore the psychological aspect on the hawk as well as on ourselves, for she becomes officially "sick" when, for practical purposes, there may be nothing wrong with her at all. A hawk reacts against being dosed with every fibre of its being, and it may be positively harmful if dosing causes it to vomit as it has a strong tendency to do.

Natural food contains all the vitamins and minerals that a

hawk needs, in the best possible form. No amount of artificially vitaminized and mineralized inferior food can equal it.

I suppose most of us become "bug-falconers" at some time or other, but happily for ourselves as well as our hawks the phase does not usually last very long, because always there comes a day when our over-solicitude does actual harm and we are brought up with a jolt into realizing how profitless it all is. The young falconer starts off all right thinking no evil in regard to disease, he is too preoccupied in mastering the rudiments of Falconry for that. However as he becomes more proficient his mind becomes more enquiring and he looks round for possible trouble. His search does not have to go very far, for two little devils are ready to spring up and shake him by the hand. They are named capillariasis and coccidiosis. They speedily fascinate him and at the same time pepper his fascination with fear. He collects hawk mutes, where formerly he was only anxious to be rid of them, packs them carefully and sends them away for microscopic examination. More often than not the report which he duly receives states that his hawk has one or both of the diseases. The typed sheet of notepaper in his hands all at once becomes a grim pronouncement, for his hawk, which until now had apparently been in good health, suddenly becomes in his mind a creature stricken by disease. His pleasant anticipation of happy hawking days is now clouded by the bacterial peril. His whole world of Falconry now seems insecure under the threat. In contemplating the

175

situation I am reminded of Alan Porter's little poem called

THE WHITE CAT

The fire whispered to the old white cat:

I shall grow fat.

Out in the night I'll jump, and there

Swallow up the air.

I shall take trees and mountain-tops for tinder

Till the whole world's a cinder.

Alarmed, the young falconer procures powerful drugs and pushes them down his hawk's throat. The wretched bird is watched by the hour for fear she should vomit the stuff, so entirely foreign to her constitution, which she generally succeeds in doing for all his (to her hostile) efforts to force her to keep it down. After failure the poor bird is probably subjected to the same treatment the next day, so that training or hawking is halted.

The pity of it is that, whereas coccidiosis and capillariasis do not necessarily harm the hawk (wild hawks certainly are not immune), the drugs may very well do so. I once so killed a fine passager. Previously there had been nothing wrong with her appearance, certainly not with her performance, but not content to leave well alone I started to look round the corner for trouble and found it in a report that she had capillariasis.

The drug I forced her to swallow killed her, but it cured me forever of being a "bug-falconer."

To-day if my hawk stretches out her neck and gapes wide her beak in a voiceless announcement that she has worms, or if a friend whispers his fear that coc. or cap. may get the better of her, I call to mind the last two lines of the already mentioned poem:

Still dozing by the fireside sat
The old white cat.

and I commend that attitude of mind to any young falconer, should he read these lines, who finds it hard to control his fear of what disease might do to his hawk.

If there is an inverted satisfaction in trying to cure aggressive disease there is a positive satisfaction in taking steps to prevent it. By constant watchfulness and attention to detail we can confidently expect a large measure of success in maintaining the health of hawks, whereas success rarely attends the falconer's efforts to cure disease when it has made its onslaught.

Yet in the maintenance of health there is another pitfall that should be avoided. I refer to that excess of zeal wherein a falconer tries to make good hawks still better. I have given antibiotics to nestling Peregrines to make them grow bigger. The result was not what I had hoped. The birds might have grown larger if their digestions had not been taxed by the foreign substance they had to swallow with their food. For a long time I found it hard to believe that hawks would not benefit by a dosage of vitamin substitutes. If they tasted the stuff before swallowing, nature made them instantly reject it. By subterfuge I succeeded in getting a young Gyrfalcon to swallow two drops of Cod Liver Oil with her food for a few days. She had been badly taken from the nest and was minus four tail feathers which had been replaced by deformities, otherwise her health was perfect. I thought the extra vitamins might help her tail. Then after one such meal the oil made her retch the whole contents of her crop up. Further efforts to make her take food, without oil, were unsuccessful and she began to look sick. I became alarmed and feared she was going to develop inflamed crop. To my great relief she took, and kept down, a small quantity of food before sundown and the situation was saved. I discontinued the oil and felt better for it. I am sure she did. Later, without artificial aids she grew four normal tail feathers.

The basic need for good health is correct feeding. Given that, and everything else being equal, a hawk is most unlikely to catch the diseases of which such a frighteningly long list is given in some Falconry books. An exception to that is frounce, a disease that does sometimes strike young hawks in particular. It takes the form of cheesy deposits in the mouth and throat, and is a killer. Its scientific name is Trichomonas galliæ. Some books recommend scraping the affected parts and dressing with nitrate of silver, a treatment very painful to the patient and worse than useless. I have tried other remedies but without good effect. Dr. Robert M. Stabler of the Falconry Club of America announces, in the October 1953 issue of their Journal, the discovery of a cure in a compound manufactured by the Lederle Laboratories of the American Cyanimid Company, sold under the trade name of Enheptin. It is recommended that the drug be administered in gelatin capsules gently pushed down into the crop. The dose is given daily for a week, for a sparrow-hawk 10 mg., a Peregrine tiercel 20 mg., a falcon 25 mg., and a Gyrfalcon 50 mg. I have heard of these doses being given twice daily. In Britain the drug is manufactured by Messrs. May and Baker Ltd., and is sold under the name of Entramin, and an obliging chemist can be persuaded to make it up into capsules. American Falconers claim it as an infallible cure. Hawks apparently have no difficulty in keeping it down.

Pigeons get frounce. Pigeon fanciers call it canker. It appears that hawks become infected from that source, so that Prevention dictates that we discontinue using pigeons as food, but as they are so readily available it would be difficult to rule them out altogether. For my part I take comfort in the thought that frounce has never struck any Peregrine of mine once it has become hard-penned after outgrowing the nestling stage. So I shall continue to use domestic pigeons as food— with discretion, being extra careful to reject any that show any suspicion of disease.

In my early days my hawks sometimes suffered from corns and swollen feet. I have little doubt now that butchers' meat was a contributory cause because I have never had a case since I gave up this unsuitable food. Cage birds, too, get somewhat similar foot trouble when given food lacking in certain vitamins that they require. That butchers' meat lacks certain vitamins and minerals necessary for hawks is proved by the fact that it makes wrecks of growing nestlings. What virtually kills young birds cannot be ideal for adults.

If a man tries to maintain his hawks on butchers' meat and rabbit he will be pretty often up against the various forms of disease as listed in Hawking books, and others that are not. The nutritional value of rabbit is poor and if he persist in rationing a hawk on it he is almost certain to run into trouble. It is under such conditions that worms, capillariasis and coccidiosis get a grip on the hawk. On unsuitable food a hawk's feet are unnaturally pale and her feathers are ragged, lustreless and brittle. Could anyone ignore these signs of disease? Compare a hawk so treated with one that is fed on natural food. The latter carries the signs of health in its richly coloured feet and bright, full eye. Its plumage lies close and shines like burnished steel.

Leaving aside such major issues let us pass on to carelessness in little matters, such as dropping food about, which can lead to trouble. Beginners are the worst offenders in this respect, probably because they have so many other things to think about. They are apt to leave a trail of food fragments on the weathering ground, some of them to be discovered days or even weeks later in a stinking condition and eaten by hungry hawks. Then they may wonder why a hawk gets inflammation of the crop! It is an unforgivable oversight. So, too, is the shedding of food fragments on the mews floor. Hawks cannot get at them, but if they can see them the following morning they may spend themselves in much harmful bating in their efforts to do so, and the falconer, on entering, may wonder why their wings are drooping, their mouths open, and their feet hot.

I believe that a hawk's health benefits inestimably if she breathe the same fresh air inside the mews that she gets outside. In the summer months a few falconers leave their hawks out to weather during the nights. I have done it myself with young eyasses that were not being hacked and that were not muscular enough for it to be safe to tie them on the screen-perch in the mews. But I believe it is a practice that should be discontinued as soon as they become sufficiently strong and steady for them to be taken in at night. Jowking on their blocks at a height that no free hawk would choose they cannot escape the cold damp that the nights bring out of the ground. With the light of dawn they seek to escape their discomfort so they bate onto the dew-soaked grass. All this adds up to bodily ill-humours which produce the green mutes round their blocks. These in themselves should be sufficient warning that this treatment is not in the best interests of good health.

MISCELLANY

AS a bate from the fist is never anything less than a mishap, and should be regarded as such, it behoves the falconer to ease the hawk's sense of frustration at the unfortunate moment as much as he can. No good falconer ever blinks or turns his head until it is over, as if he were the injured party and not the hawk.

There is a right way and a wrong way to "bate" a hawk—if a bate cannot be avoided (and how often it can!). To begin with the wrist and forearm must not be held rigidly, for to do so is to make the hawk's efforts in regaining the fist twice as difficult as they need be. It makes of a bate an unnecessarily cruel performance. At the instant of the hawk's springing from the fist the forearm must yield, but no more than to put a brake on her precipitation. That reduces the shock and the sudden strain on her legs, so that she is in better shape to make the about turn and regain the fist, which she will do, lightly and easily, particularly if her muscles are hardened by much flying. Many young eyasses, whose muscles are still soft, will require additional assistance to the yielding of the forearm. When one of these, after precipitation, gets her head up from the hanging position, preparatory to the climb back to the fist, she will receive valuable help from the falconer if, by a deft dropping of the forearm, he gets his fist under her for her feet to grip instantly, so that she will be spared the strain to her back of the final pull-up.

To watch a man "bating" his hawk is to get a good insight into his degree of skill as a falconer. The beginner who is going to be any good will be anxious to get this part right. I hardly expect that he will get the knack by reading these directions, but after acquiring it he will understand the drift of them. By then he will know what it is to control a bate by the dexterity and perfect timing that it calls for. One has only to observe the effort that taxes a very young hawk to regain the insensate object that is the screen-perch to appreciate the full extent of the strain that the fist can and must save, and, incidentally, to appreciate why the falconer must arrange his mews so that there will be no bating.

Reverse the picture of a beginner in Falconry helping his hawk, with great concentration, when she is in a bate, to a scene that I witnessed some years ago. A schoolboy, new in Falconry, was "manning" his very new eyass. He was sitting on the ground by his hawk's block. The day was fine and he was enjoying the sunshine. His hawk should have been too, but she was not, for she was making repeated attempts to fly onto her nearby block, as naturally she would do. She would have done the same even if she had been held comfortably which was not the case, for the boy's fist was all upturned fingers and thumb. At every bate he thrust his fist into the air, not troubling to turn his head, satisfied that he was keeping her flapping wings clear of the ground. Everything was all right, so he thought, he was "manning" her, and the bates were nothing more than indications of this.

That boy was making three serious mistakes. Firstly, he should never carry a hawk within sight of some object onto which she wants to fly. Secondly, when she bated he offered her no assistance. Thirdly, the incline of his forearm not only increased her difficulty in regaining the fist, but the angle of forty-five degrees that he held it at made it impossible for her to avoid smacking his forearm with her wing.

It sometimes happens, fortunately not often, that a hawk in a hanging bate will make no effort to regain the fist. This means either that she does it through temper or because she believes that by flying hard towards the ground she will eventually get there. In either case it is not difficult to determine the cause. If temper, the only thing to do is to wait patiently until tiredness makes her come up. She will not repeat it often. If it is because she wants to reach the ground, the falconer, rather than let her exhaust herself, will uncoil the leash from his fist and allow her to alight on the turf. Experience soon teaches her that greater facility is available to regain the fist than to reach the ground.

If a hawk has a prolonged hanging bate and it is not convenient to let her gain the ground it is better to act rather than to let her exhaust herself. Flatten the right hand, place it behind her back, take her weight and bring her up to the vertical position breast towards you on the outside of fist. But always release the hand on the instant her feet grip the fist. The movement is done firmly but gently and with sufficient speed to give her no time to resist the hand. Above all fhe hand must not grip. Hawks intensely dislike being held on the back below where the wings join the body.

When a hawk has become reasonably steady it is good to unhood her before putting her down on the block. This is taking her along the road towards the minimum use of the hood, a goal one should keep in mind having regard to the fact that, ultimately, the hood's sole use is to keep a hawk from bating while taking her from one place to another. Obviously the more handling the falconer can give his hawk without the hood the more familiar she will become with him. The habit of making her wear it simply to suit one's own little personal conveniences is an abuse that suppresses in some degree the strengthening of cordial relationship between bird and man. We should never cease to be grateful for the fact that such a spirited creature consents to wear a hood at all. That she does so with commendable patience should make us resolved not to inflict it on her more than is necessary. If my hawk begin to show signs of impatience at wearing the hood for longer than what she has become accustomed to accept as her fair share of time I would not reproach myself for not having broken her in to a greater accommodation of my convenience. She may protest for the nonce, but I would prefer to have it that way than to have subjugated her to the extent that she would be prepared to go on wearing it indefinitely like a stuffed bird. The point is of course that in a hawk one has taken into partnership a living creature with feelings. She is not just an insensate instrument of the chase to be taken out of the hood in the manner that one takes a gun out of its case.

So when you arrive at the block unhood your hawk. Then slowly and gently unwind the leash from the glove. She soon becomes used to this little attention and will show appreciation of having her head uncovered by taking in the scene. Get her onto the block before she begins to show any uneasiness at remaining on your fist. If she rouse without waiting to be put on the block you have made a gain in taming her.

Of course no one would be so foolish as to carry out this exercise on a hawk that is not ready for it yet, but, if she is, a useful bit of manning would be missed if she were just put down in the hooded state. The few minutes spent in leisurely transferring her from fist to block unhooded, is a type of carrying that does her good because her interest is held. On principle it is right, too, because falconer and hawk should share current proceedings as much as possible This is impossible when she is just passive through being hooded.

For the sake of safety always wind the leash tidily away after taking up a hawk. It suits the hawk's convenience if it be wound round the lower three fingers, well into the knuckles so that it will not slip off. Do not include the first finger because the leash's protuberance would interfere with the comfort of her grip on the glove, and, in this connection, it is well to remember that there is only one way to make the gloved fist a comfortable perching place, and that is to keep the thumb and first finger on top, on a level. It is dangerous to let the leash hang in loops from the glove because a bating hawk may easily get a wing through one of them. In putting an unhooded hawk down on the block do not worry her by any manipulations of the fist, simply hold the glove against the block so that her feet are on a lower level than its top. She will step up to it.

If, in putting down an unhooded hawk on her block, she anticipate you by flying to it, the one thing not to do is to prevent her. To prevent her is to put her in a bate for which there is no justification whatever. To prevent her is to impose an unnecessary restriction. The whole art of training a hawk is to reduce restrictions to the minimum and to disguise the necessary ones. Far from checking her understandable impulse to fly down to her block the falconer should encourage what so often amounts to a light-hearted frolic by having the leash unwound in readiness. It is a harmless little amusement which some hawks enjoy so much that, when they are carried out of the mews unhooded. it becomes necessary not to let them see their blocks until within "leash range." Hawks that are granted this little privilege are generally quicker to perform with zest the reverse action, *i.e.*, the jump from block to fist, than are those embarrassed, puzzled, and crabbed creatures belonging to the falconer with the over-restraining hand.

A hawk will not be tempted to fly from fist to block until she has reached a degree of familiarity with the falconer. But in any case for the first time or two she may bate, not necessarily from panic but simply through nervousness at being presented with a new situation. This occasions another test of a falconer's perspicacity. On the principle that a bate on the ground is much less upsetting than a bate from the fist he will have uncoiled the leash and taken hold of its end in anticipation, so that if the hawk should spring from his fist she will not hang but, instead, will come down on the ground the length of the leash away. There she will bate, even so the bate will be eased by the play of the falconer's left hand on the leash while he ties the end, with his right, to the block. The one thing that he will *not* do is to pin the hawk to the ground by holding down the swivel at the end of her jesses. This frightens a hawk badly because it makes her feel trapped.

The reader may think that I have laboured a lot of the foregoing with too much detail. I plead that it is the detail of handling and managing a hawk wherein lie her nascent impressions of him for good or ill. And remember that from the very first she is the severest of critics of everything that he does, and no wonder, for in the whole of man's excursions into the training of wild creatures there is no other instance where

189

trainer and trainee are in such close and constant rapport.

A hooded hawk may be taken onto the fist by raising her middle toe with the bare hand and pushing the glove under it. Her entire foot then takes hold and is followed by the other one. Alternatively the glove may be gently pressed against the back of her legs when she will step back onto it. Some falconers use the latter method for getting an unhooded hawk onto the fist. It is not necessary and personally I think it looks a bit odd to see the gloved fist fumbling under the hawk's tail, because she will very readily step forward onto it of her own free will when accustomed to do so. The "back-of-the-legs" method relies on automatic reaction. I dislike to see an unhooded hawk so tricked onto the glove. In raising this point I claim that it is not the triviality that it may appear to be, it serves as a reminder of a cardinal principle in training, *i.e.*, that the hawk be encouraged to take the initiative in every way possible that will lead to the strengthening of her ties of familiarity with man. Stepping voluntarily onto the fist is the first small gesture she makes in her willingness to come more than half way to meet him. That willingness is seen in its full perfection when she strains at the end of the leash to get to him, impatient for his outstretched fist.

A hawk's mind works at a speed that can be divined by the born falconer. He will take her along no faster than what her mind works. He knows exactly what pace to set when walking outside with—say—a timorous goshawk on his fist. His movements, in themselves, will add nothing to the fearful impressions that assail her from the sight of unfamiliar things.

When he brings his gos into the mews again, he knows, without having to remind himself of it, that her previous confused impressions outside leave her in an instant when she finds herself again under the familiar roof. He knows, without having to see it in her eye, that a single thought is rapidly gathering speed in her head. She wants to regain her perch and the sense of comparative security that the feel of it, under her feet, gives her. If an indifferent austringer were carrying her she would of course bate to reach it, and that accident would not perturb him. But the man we are now watching has his mind attuned to his hawk's. She has bated, unavoidably, during his walk outside, but in the mews here at least she can be controlled. With his fist held high he loses no time in getting her well above the perch while he prepares her leash for subsequent tying thereto. As he lowers her he spreads his elbows over each side of the perch, lengthwise, to forestall her attempting to jump the few inches down to it. When the leash is in position for tying he lets her step forward, gratefully, onto the perch, and his left forearm resting horizontally on it will forestall her straining at the end of her jesses on that side, while his spread right hand prevents her doing likewise on the other. It is all done so smoothly, and his hawk has been set to rest with never a flutter to mar the proceedings.

That hawk has been skilfully steered to her anchorage over the smooth water of efficient management. Nothing had happened to remind her that she was tied to the man. Thus does he continually study her mind so that he can smooth the path of her. training by directing her inclinations the right way.

The other fellow puts the cart before the horse because he tries to cope with a lively and wayward bundle of feathers before considering a delicately balanced mind.

This reminds me of some correspondence I have had with certain leading American falconers, from whom I believe we could learn much. Mr. Harold Webster, of Wheatridge, Colorado, has the startling statement to make that he hates the word "training," because it is too easily confounded with the idea of pushing a hawk through metaphorical hoops, at every stage, until finally it reach the open arena where only the blandishments of food can preserve a tenuous remote control. That is the substance of Mr. Webster's remarks and we would do well to digest it mentally. He goes on to state, in so many words, that a falconer who knows his business does not "train" his hawk, but leads her all the way until she discloses herself. There I think he hits the nail exactly on the head.

Some falconers claim to be able to identify a first-class hawk by appearance alone. In some instances such judgment has been proved correct. Personally I have no faith in my own ability in this direction; but as the years go by one does begin to associate certain characteristics, in the early days of training, with what seemingly promises to be a hawk of above-average qualities. Thus if she bate lightly and is up again on the fist in one movement, if, in feeding her, she consume her food faster than what suits your planning, I, for one, would expect her to turn out to be a hawk of above-average performance.

Under this chapter heading it seems that I can write anything; so to these wandering remarks I would like to add a word about packing a hawk for a journey. A hessian-lined basket seems to be the conventional way of doing this and it is not without its advantages. But it has serious disadvantages too. A hawk gets her talons into the sides, and even the top, where she hangs and flaps to the danger of breaking her feathers. The lid seldom fits the body of the basket snugly, so that light penetrates round the edge, and it is to this light at the top that the imprisoned hawk keeps jumping and falling back onto her tail. A circular, wooden hat-box type container, with smooth sides and no hessian, except that which is fixed securely on the bottom in several thicknesses into which she can get a firm hold with her feet, is the ideal, but a rectangular box, with angle strips let into the inside corners, is nearly as good. To ensure the minimum amount of restiveness all ventilation holes should be well under the level of the hawk's eye. These should be sufficiently small so that she will get no clear view of all the frightening things that go on outside of her temporary prison.

When straightening feathers that have been bent never use scalding water as this destroys their nature and makes them brittle.

THE GYRFALCON

PART of this chapter appeared in the Journal of The British Falconers' Club. My thanks are due to the Editor for permission to republish. The emendations are the result of knowledge gained from increased experience.

The appearance of the Gyi falcon calls less for descriptive generalizations than the bare statement that everything about her bespeaks strength and speed. Whereas the Peregrine is more delicately suggestive of those two qualities the Gyr figures them with arresting boldness. On the block she stands to attention with power focused on the great breadth of her back and in the great breadth across the hunched prominence of her wing butts. The emphasis of her strength and speed is in her weighty upper-half. So much for her physique. As to her expression it is more variable than the Peregrines. She has the latter's nobility but there are times when she sits her block when it is positively of a frowning arrogance. That is how she appears when taken unawares. On sight of the falconer it changes instantly to match the varying moods that could be expected against a background of familiarity.

In character Gyrs differ considerably from Peregrines. This speaks of eyasses for I have partly trained only one haggard and that had all of the Peregrine's aloofness which the eyass

Gyr has not. In regard to her relationship with man I see no difference between the Gyr that has been taken up after a month's hack and the Gyr that has had none at all. They are equally aggressively tame. The hacked Gyr has none of the reserve of the hacked Peregrine. She does not go wild at hack. If the Peregrine has any affection for man she rarely shows it. Gyrs have none of that kind of pride, they are affectionate and demonstrate it unreservedly, the falcons more so than the tiercels, generally speaking. Often their affection for their owner resembles that of a dog. Thus, when approached on the block, even when they have a full crop, they often jump down to fawn at one's feet. Extend the gloved fist and they are on it in a flash. If I lie on the grass by my Norway Gyrfalcon's block she cannot stay there but must come down and play with the buttons and folds of my clothing.

Playfulness is a strong characteristic. What eyass Peregrine wants to play with man as many eyass Gyrs do? In this, and in other respects, their enthusiasm in their relationship with man matches that of dogs to a surprising degree. One is reminded of it in the honest welcome they give one when entering the mews. Whereas the Peregrine preserves her calm dignity on the perch the Gyr cranes forward, all impatient for the fist. And in the weathering enclosure they sometimes greet one's approach straining and jumping at the end of the leash just as a dog would. Neither do they confine their excitement to such physical exhibitions for they let go their voices. You can condemn it as screaming if you like, but I for one cannot find it in me to object to such vociferous cheerfulness, there is nothing mean in it.

Great tameness is so much a characteristic of the Gyrfalcons that the other side of their nature stands out all the more by contrast. They are very easily upset. Anything that would make a Peregrine slightly nervous sends a Gyr into a panic. They suffer too from unreasoning fear and bate madly at nothing at all. Some are worse than others but they all share this unfortunate trait in some degree. The tiercels are particularly "electric."

Leaving out of account such senseless hysteria the intelligence of Gyrs goes beyond that of Peregrines. Or it may be that it is manifested more because it is more on the surface while the Peregrine keeps hers deeper within her. However this may be there are times when the Gyr's intelligence causes inconvenience. As an instance of this they resent being hooded in the middle of a meal. It is easy to hood a Peregrine while she is feeding, at the most she accepts the hood with a mental shrug of the shoulders. But to a Gyr the intrusion of the hood at meal-time is unwarrantable interference, and unless care is taken she is quick to foot it out of the hand. It is not only that but the affronted look they give one which is different from anything I have seen in a Peregrine. Falcons especially get really angry and raise their hackles as if threatening violence if you do not behave yourself. To give them their due they are prepared to accept it as nicely as could be at all other times for then they are very easy to hood, accepting this necessity with sweet reasonableness. But their unwillingness to be hooded until they have satisfied their hunger puts the falconer in a quandary when he wants to ration them. He can persist with the hood, of course, and he will probably get it on and they will go on feeding in it, but on the other hand there may be a scene and that must be avoided. In any case they dislike what they regard as its untimely use, and experience teaches that the best results are to be obtained from a Gyr when the partnership is kept as far as possible on a fifty-fifty basis. "I will wear the hood all right to please you," she says, "but be a good fellow and don't bother me with it while I am feeding." So I let her take all she wants to eat before hooding her. This means that she cannot be flown twice within the hour, but she will accommodate the falconer to the extent that she will take a small feed in the morning and another one in the evening. In that way she can be flown twice daily and I find that this practice works out satisfactorily.

A Gyrfalcon weighs around three pounds nine or ten ounces and the tiercel a pound less. They are greedy feeders only at certain times but in the main they eat proportionately less than do Peregrines. They can be kept in perfect health and free from surfeit on the quickly digested meat of rabbit and chicken. Too much rabbit lowers their vitality. They need a certain amount of chicken (bird) fat to preserve the gloss and elasticity of their feathers. They moult perfectly on chicken, rabbit, and an occasional grey squirrel. They commence to moult the middle of April and have their last flight feather down by the beginning of October, which is the same as Peregrines.

In recommending chicken as food I refer, of course, to light-breed cockerels which are unsuitable for table purposes. As day-old chicks they can be practically begged from the hatcheries and cheaply reared on a free range. They can be killed from the age of ten weeks. When fully-grown they begin to put on too much fat to be good for hawks, so then the falconer must eat them himself. Heavy breeds put on too much breast meat and hawks do not relish chicken breast. In Britain Gyrs undoubtedly need food of a less rich quality than they do up north. It must be remembered that in their native habitat they quite often miss a day's feed when weather conditions prevent their hunting, so, when not moulting, it is good to withhold food altogether on occasional days, such as when the weather makes hawking impossible.

All the evidence that I have collected goes to show that fresh air, day and night, is a primary necessity. On the other hand it does them no good to be left outside at night on their blocks, if the green mutes then produced are to be taken as warning. So, for the night, I recommend a high perch in a dry, open-fronted mews with screened opening.

They must never be allowed to get overheated. When a

summer's sun is high in the sky they need not only shade, but deep shade.

For a long time Gyrs have had the reputation of being exceedingly difficult to keep in health. Indeed it was the experience of falconers in the last century, as it has been in this, that they soon die. Only within recent years has it been discovered that the common cause of death is feeding them on pigeons.

I used to believe that the rich flesh of pigeon was too heating for them in a temperate climate, and certainly the post mortem examination seemed to support this belief because, in every case, a congested liver was reported. I found that even one feed of pigeon could cause death. Since I discontinued giving this food not a single Gyr in my care has died.

I had found out how to keep Gyrs alive and healthy but my discovery was far short of complete. For the rest I have to thank Colonel Meredith, the president of the Falconry Club of America, who has taught me that it is not the pigeon flesh, in itself, that kills a Gyr but the disease that a pigeon may carry, and that disease is Trichomonas gallinæ, or our old enemy frounce.

This being so it is a remarkable fact that, when frounce from this source attacks a Gyr, the familiar symptom of cheesy encrustations in the mouth and throat is absent. The first indication of the disease is in loss of appetite, although the hawk appears hungry on seeing food. If, after two or three days, the mutes become blue, small and frequent, it used to be an unfailing warning to me that the bird was doomed. Forty-eight hours later her breathing quickens ; and a couple of days after that she is dead. So swiftly does flounce kill a Gyr, whereas a Peregrine will survive for weeks. In short its manifestation has nothing in common between the two species. The Peregrine does not even share the early loss of appetite.

Colonel Meredith's Jerkin once had this disease, but he cured him with a six-day course of Enheptin, or Entramin as it is named over here (see chapter on Health). He dosed his hawk twice daily, each capsule containing 50 mg. of the drug. Having thus recovered from the disease it appears that a Gyr gains some degree of immunity, at least Meredith informs me that he continues to give his bird pigeon. Such is his confidence in this cure that he feels he has nothing to fear even if the disease should reappear.

I suspect that frounce does not always make its onslaught in chronic form, and that it sometimes gets no further than temporary loss of appetite. In this condition a Gyr is skating on very thin ice, as only one bate that gets her out of breath is sufficient to plunge her into the full malignancy of the disease.

Even with the cure permanently at hand it will be thought by many that it is best to remove the root cause of the disease by not feeding pigeon (even woodpigeons are sometimes carriers of T. gallinæ). Since adopting this policy my Gyrs have not manifested the first stage of the disease in loss of appetite.

Granted that the cure is infallible I still prefer to hold to the principle that giving hawks potions is to be avoided whenever possible, especially when dealing with nestlings whose growth of body and feather can hardly support this sort of interference.

Gyrs have a reputation for easily getting bad feet. I have never taken any precaution against this, no soft turfs for them to sit on or anything like that, and I have never had a case of it, doubtless because I do not feed butchers' meat which predisposes this condition.

Having regard to the natural tameness of these falcons a falconer might suppose that they would be correspondingly easy to train. Unfortunately this is not the case. By comparison the Peregrine is easily led by man. He prescribes a programme of training for her and she goes ahead in it with little or no trouble. The Gyr however has too many ideas of her own to which she gives priority over the falconer's. When an eyass Peregrine, in training, is put on the wing the falconer can confidently expect her to return to the lure, but it is a matter for congratulation when you get your young Gyr back during the first few weeks. It is not that she flies around ignoring the lure, because she is seldom within the area to see it. From this the conclusion might be drawn that she is more likely to be lost than not. The danger of course does exist, yet she has a most disconcerting way of returning to the falconer an hour or two after release. During her absence she has probably covered an alarming extent of country. And so this "chuck and chance it" game continues to fray the nerves while the falconer despairs of achieving anything in the way of training. However ravenously hungi y she may be when she leaves the fist her early return to the lure cannot be relied upon, and so for weeks she remains a law unto herself. If hacked in one place and afterwards flown in another she probably would be lost. If not hacked she is quick to learn the landmarks of the area in which she is first flown and there is then a fair chance of her not being lost. Thanks to her intelligence it is easy to teach her to "home." But the greatest safeguard is to hack her in the area in which she is to be flown at quarry. Hack is necessary for Gyrs for without it, unlike Peregrines, they do not seem to develop fully their lungs, so that they get out of breath and become tired, after special exertions, before they ought to, and time does not appear to correct this.

From the foregoing I hope it will be appreciated what a burden of anxiety and trouble an eyass can give one. What a passager or haggard would do to one I hardly dare imagine. With the eyass the most a talconer can hope for, in her first season, is that he does not lose her. If he manage to kill a few head of quarry with her he will be very lucky. If he end up the season with nothing in the score book but with a trained and steady hawk he will have accomplished something for which he should be profoundly thankful.

From that last remark it may be gathered that the twentieth century Gyr can be trained. Indeed she can. If the falconer press on through disappointment and despair he will find his crooked path becoming straighter. Gyrs can not only be brought under control, but can be brought to a degree of training and steadiness before the end of their first season that compares favourably with anything that Peregrines can show. Indeed, after they have passed their first season's basic training, it can be said that eyass Gyrs are less likely to be lost than Peregrines. This can partly be explained by the fact that your. Gyr is not likely to meet a wild one, whereas the steadiest Peregrine, flown over the same ground year after year, is almost certain to be led astray sometime by a wild one of the opposite sex. I should add the rider that a cast of Gyrs, flown together, are very likely to stray. Indeed if one be flown separately, and left out, it would be most unwise to put the second on the wing before the first has been taken up.

During the autumn and winter months Gyrs apparently are not affected by a migration urge, but it probably would be dangerous to fly them in March, April and May.

When the young Gyr has finished sowing all her wild oats when by prudence gentleness and patience you have persuaded her finally to accept her role as man's ally, she will delight you with that intelligent companionship that, above all other hawks, she alone can show. She gives you obedience that has little or no connection with the whip-lash of hunger, but of the generous kind that bespeaks her contentment with the life that has brought you and her together. I have compared her temperament with that of a dog's, and I find I cannot get away from the comparison, for, whereas the Peregrine, however tame, always guards those certain reservations that defy our penetration, the Gyr, more particularly the Gyrfalcon, gives you the whole of her heart and mind. One illustration will suffice to show what I mean. It may be said that the lure is the emblem of the trained Peregrine in the field. When flying a falcon, even one old in the service of man, you would not like to be without it, would you ? But with the Gyr it becomes dispensable. Blow the whistle and she comes in straight to pitch at your feet, to look for the outstretched fist. Such obedience, however, has nothing of servility in it. She comes to you because she backs your decision that "Time's up," but I would be dishonest if I did not add that she has her own ideas in such matters. Thus, while beating a part of the moor, she uses her own intelligence to assess the likelihood of the presence of grouse, and it sometimes happens that she decides that there are none to be found before your own patience becomes exhausted, then she comes to your feet in her time and not yours. You can order her up again, but her decision is final, and there is nothing to be done but give in to her. If you do not she will follow you closely until you do. Whereas a Peregrine would as soon go her independent way as suffer any argument with the falconer over the question of her return to him. This further illustrates that, far from being servile, the Gyr insists on a fifty fifty basis in her partnership with man, and if you protest that such intelligence fools the falconer I can only reply that you cannot have it every way.

I have never yet flown a Gyr that did not show willingness to wait-on, but it has not yet been my luck to have one to wait-on really high, although on occasions they have flown at tremendous heights, climbing with less effort than Peregrines. In waiting-on they show a keener appreciation of the purpose of this exercise. With Peregrines one has to allow for a certain amount of drift, but all the time Gyrs keep in tenaciously to the dogs, hovering directly over them at times like a kestrel. Indeed in their anxiety not to miss the first sign of any movement of feather down below they fly with their heads over their backs, when their tails are towards the dogs, so that not for an instant are their eyes off the main chance.

When a Peregrine stoops from a high waiting-on pitch one gets the impression of her falling, falling, falling. Only when she flattens out from her descent does she appear to drive right onto the quarry. A Gyr's stoop has more thrust in it, she drives right down her descent. Her towering throw-up at the end of it indicates the greater weight of the impetus behind her stoop. When her quarry is squarely hit it is not likely to get up again, but the grouse, cunning bird that it is, often endeavours to seek the safety of the ground with that of speedy travel through the air by flying off with its breast almost brushing the heather. In that way a hawk cannot deliver a body blow without serious risk to herself. Consequently her hind talons only skim the grouse's back so that it receives no injury worth mentioning. Whether it is bowled over or not it flies again, with undiminished speed, towards the nearest patch of bracken. It is just at this stage when a hawk's speed, on the level, really counts. Ordinarily the Peregrine and the grouse are pretty evenly matched. The former is the faster of the two when going down-wind, but nearly always gets left behind when going up-wind. After being floored a grouse always has the sense to fly up-wind. So, in this race for the bracken we look with anxious eyes to the Gyr with her tradition of great speed.

Are Gyrfalcons really as fast as what the books represent them to be ? It has never been my good fortune to fly a Greenlander, but I have flown Icelanders and Norwegians. Of the last two I think perhaps the Icelander is the faster bird. I am certain that no Norwegian that I have flown was more than half as fast again as a Peregrine, probably less. The most that an observer could say was that they were appreciably faster. A Gyrfalcon is a bit slow to recover from her throw-up, a bit slow to get back into top speed, and the result is that by the time she catches up again with her quarry it often reaches the cover of bracken. But after a Jerkin has grazed his grouse and bowled it into the heather he whips into it again at a speed that gives the grouse little chance to fly very far. So, at the end of the season his score is greater than hers. In writing this I am referring to the particular moor over which I hawk where encroaching acres of deep bracken have spoilt the chance of the best Peregrines in building up a decent score. A Gyrfalcon, for the reason given above, loses most of her quarry in bracken, but on the occasions when she does pursue a grouse over wide-open moor her great speed soon wears it down. So much faster is she than a Peregrine that it is obvious to anyone watching the flight that, even up-wind, the quarry is completely in her power.

I have seen a Gyrfalcon's superior power of flight well exemplified in flights against wild Peregrines. However high these pass over my moor my Norwegian Gyrfalcon, now in her fourth season, cannot resist going up to do battle with them. The spectator marvels at the ease of her steep and swift ascent. Straight up on her tail she climbs until she gets above the intruder. The latter appears to be about as helpless against her attack as a sheep before a sheep-dog. There is hardly any opposition before the Peregrine yields to evasive flight and seeks only escape, with the result that she is forced down to ground level: In two instances such flights were seen to end with the Peregrine taking refuge in bracken or heather.

To say that eyass Gyrs should be hacked is an understatement. They *must* be hacked, otherwise forever afterwards they will suffer from shortage of breath. Unhacked Peregrines quickly get over this disability but unhacked Gyrs never do. Apart from this there is another equally strong consideration to be taken into account. Unhacked Gyrs do not take life seriously enough. Mention has been made early in this chapter of their playfulness. Their love of fun can be amusing in its proper place, but in the field it is the very devil. The stark fact is that they do not take their hawking seriously, and I would not put it past a few hacked individuals to show some signs, occasionally, of this weakness. But, keeping to the unhacked Gyr, one moment she has the whole field enraptured by a superb exhibition of flying, and in the next she makes a fool of the falconer in front of the onlookers by purposely letting go the grouse she has caught. Anyone might think that this vice would disappear with age, but it does not. Therefore the lesson to be learnt from this is to hack eyass Gyrs for as long as possible.

Mr. Morlan Nelson of Idaho, U.S.A., who has had more experience and more success with Gyrs than any other living falconer, traps them a month or more after leaving the eyrie. Thus at the outset he starts with the very best advantage. They have had natural hack, arc as wild as can be when caught, and yet have not had sufficient experience in killing for themselves for them to be put in the class of passagers with the accompanying risk of losing them. His famous Gyrfalcon "Tundra" is one of these. She waits-on so high that he has to use field-glasses, on occasion, to keep her in sight. To quote from his letters—"Tundra is flying in great style and is a wonderful falcon for any quarry . . ." "She leaves all falcons in the dust when it comes to flying, being in a class that will always be singular to the species."

To sum up, it may be said that, for over a century, the Gyr has been eclipsed in Falconry, but from the knowledge gained in recent years we have recovered at least some of the lost art in maintaining her in health and managing her in the field. She is a creature of contrasts, and, in our present state of knowledge, more difficult to train than our old friend the Peregrine. But I am not alone in the belief that a Gyrfalcon, or Gyrtiercel, successfully flown is by far the most rewarding experience a falconer can have.